MW01711223

The Crystal Road

JAN-ANDREA DAY

The Crystal Road
Copyright © 2018 by Jan-Andrea Day

No part of this publication may be reproduced, distributed, or transmitted in any form or by any means, including photocopying, recording, or other electronic or mechanical methods, without the prior written permission of the author, except in the case of brief quotations embodied in critical reviews and certain other non-commercial uses permitted by copyright law.

tellwell

Tellwell Talent
www.tellwell.ca

ISBN
978-1-77370-813-3 (Hardcover)
978-1-77370-812-6 (Paperback)
978-1-77370-814-0 (eBook)

Table of Contents

To my children, Abby and Ian.
May you grow to be strong, positive, happy and
appreciative of the little things in life.

Preface

This has been a healing journey that began with my childhood journals. There are so many factors that influence who we become and what choices that we make. Experiences can be moments of joy or regret, and some of these we remember, if we rely on memory alone. But, sometimes when we take the time to document the events of our hectic lives, some things become clearer in hindsight. Things like, fate, whether a marriage is worth fighting for, and whether life is worth living. To each of these questions, my journals have directed my choices, when faced with the hardest times of my life.

We all have a story. Anyone could write a book. I did this as a Legacy Project to explain why I am the way I am and to help me heal through the tough times. I thought it would be a better guide for my children than trying to follow my journals. The latter will be another experience for them one day.

I've always been an open, honest person, and just wanted someone to hug me, cherish me and hold my hand throughout life. I realized that a wonderful network of friends and family can fulfill all of these needs. The most difficult but worthwhile journey, is the journey within. There is a buried treasure, to be found. For me, that treasure is love, peace, and strength, and knowing that I gave it my best!

CHAPTER ONE

Just Me

I have kept a journal ever since I can remember. My first purple diary had a little lock and key and I had written in pencil in my very juvenile style of writing that looked like I was using my non-dominant hand. "Bobby gave me the bumps today." It was on my tenth birthday. The bumps were when someone could get a hold of you and knee your backside the number of times corresponding to your age, or two someones grabbing either two arms or two legs and bringing you down to tap your bottom on the ground that many times. I usually ran away to avoid the bumps. I usually ran away from Bobby, because he wanted to plant me with a slobbery kiss.

One day, he gave me a little heart shaped stone and wrote on it "Bobby loves Jan". I kept it for a while because I was so moved by the gesture. In third grade, we were the oldest kids in the school, and it was the first year that in our program of French immersion we got to have a half day in English. Our school days had been all in French until then. That was a great year, being the Seniors at Val

Caron Public School. We were the second group, to begin the new French Immersion Program in town.

For grades four to six, we went to Valley View Public School, which then offered both the Core English Program and the French immersion Program. Kristiann (Kristi) was my best friend throughout most of elementary school. She was exceptionally bright, and I always knew that if I needed a partner for anything, I could count on her. We had sleepovers and would play with her Smurf collection, or her Commodore 64 games, or with her large briefcase under her bed, in which she kept her sleuthing supplies and treasures. I envied that she had the Commodore 64 computer, whereas I had the Vic 20. I envied Kristi for many reasons, and her computer had better games than mine. Games were saved on tape cassettes. On my Vic 20, you had to press play on the special tape player connected to the computer by a cord, in order to load the software.

I was such a goody-two shoes, as I always played by my parents' rules. One day, I heard Kristi say "Shut up!". I was appalled. My parents would never let me say those words. In my world they were on the list of "bad words". And good kids don't swear. I was very disappointed with her. I briefly considered not being her friend anymore, but I forgave her and let it go. Our friendship was my safety blanket, after all.

I was pretty insecure, and always wanted to be just like everyone else. I had sandy blonde hair, blue eyes, with a touch of green, a pale complexion, and a face and body full of freckles and moles. Everyone else had such smooth uninterrupted skin. I was rather self-conscious about my beauty marks, that I would hide my arms under the table when my classmates were sitting next to me. On the bus, I would try to sit with my feet up on my toes, so that the mass of my upper legs didn't widen overly when squashed on the seat. I was by no means overweight. My parents said I looked 'healthy', but all of my friends were thinner than I was. I tried exercising. I tried the 'Fibre Trim' diet pills, that would swell in your stomach to make you feel fuller, and I tried starving myself. I didn't believe that 'healthy' was a good look for me.

My parents always bragged about my looks and intellect, but that was a part of their job. My self-confidence took a hit in sixth grade, when Kristi suddenly started to ignore me and push me away. This was devastating to eleven-year-old me. We had other friends but I hadn't invested as much in those friendships. I felt so lonely. I never knew why, perhaps I smothered her or she felt that I was holding her back. But, I regretted not having nurtured my friendships with the other girls in my class, like Shelley, Cathy, Michelle or Spring.

By grade seven, we had a new classmate named "Jody" (Jode). Jody was very slender with brown eyes and naturally reddish brown and semi curly hair. We thought she had anemia, because she had occasional fainting spells. She lived on a big property in Hanmer with her family, and they had horses. With a small class of fourteen, we all vied for Jode's attention.

Jody managed to nurture friendships with many of us. We used to talk on the phone, after school to discuss the gossip of the day. We had sleepovers and sometimes, Jody would invite us to go horseback riding. They let me ride a horse named "Princess". Princess always wanted to graze, and would not follow the others when we tried to go for a ride. I occasionally took my bicycle over to her house, but Dominion Drive was a deceivingly long road, and it made for a very long ride from Flake subdivision. I considered Jode to be my new best friend.

I liked being active, but was never very competitive. Since we were such a small group, anyone could make the school's athletic teams. My grade eight teacher, Mr. Chevrette used to call me "Reckless Abandon", for my approach to Volleyball. I was all over the court. He also made me do hurdles for the track and field meet at Laurentian University, but I knocked over a hurdle and got water on the knee. I hobbled around for weeks afterwards. The same teacher saw my determination to get excellence at the yearly spring track and field challenges, as I was tired of the same old silver badges. The year prior I had won gold, but for my last year, grade eight, I was determined to get excellence. He let me attempt the 500 metre run over and over, and for the endurance run, I pushed myself to the point of exhaustion. On the last quarter of the last lap, my legs were flailing to push me forward. I remember it as if in slow motion, just willing each leg to move forward as I swayed, and the stars came out. I was no sooner across the finish line, and I was flat on the grass, unable to open my eyes. For a hot sunny day, everything went black, and quiet. I came to with the sound of cutie pie Bobby hovering over me, and then I could speak, but I just couldn't get my eyes to open. I had heat exhaustion. Mr. Chevrette drove me home from school that day. I did get the excellence badge, though. Looking back, I think it may have been for my determination rather than my skill.

We became a group of five friends. Kristi, Jody, Shelley, Crystal and I. Crystal had skipped a grade. Kristi spoke to me occasionally, but we were never as close as we were up to the sixth grade. Mr. Chevrette, pulled us five girls aside one day near Grade eight graduation to give us a pep talk. He said he believed we would all be very successful in our endeavors. I always thought that I had a very special destiny.

I used to pray to God. And as if he could hear me from beyond, I would talk to my late Grandpa Redman whom I never had the privilege of meeting. I was comforted by the thought that he was watching over us. Sometimes, when we visited Ottawa, my Mom would take us kids to her Dad's grave. It was a flat, brown metallic, rectangular plaque upon which his name was inscribed. It was surrounded by a lush green carpet of grass with memorials interspersed.

I informed him about my life and whatever issues I had at home or friendship woes I had at that moment. My Dad always told me that I really would have loved my Mom's Father. Dad was pretty religious from his upbringing (Pentecostal and Salvation Army, or "Sally Ann"), but it was Mom, that took us to St. James' in the Valley United church, on most Sundays. We dreaded it. After I was too old for Sunday School, I didn't mind it so much. I really liked the fresh loaf of bread they would pass around and the grape juice for communion. I didn't like to sing out loud, because my voice would really waiver on those high notes, so I usually mouthed the words. My Grandmother on Mom's side, Nan, used to sing really high and shaky, like old people sing in falsetto. I felt sometimes compelled to try harder when she was next to me.

Dad was a people-person, and a loving father. He was born in Inverness, Scotland, his Mom's homeland. They moved to Newfoundland when he was two years old. That is where he grew up, in a little town called Old Shop, in Trinity Bay. He jokingly described it to be between Dildo and Spread Eagle. But, it was true. They lived right by the Ocean, in Trinity Bay. He was the third oldest of three girls and four boys. Back then, the kids worked hard to help out around the house. They didn't take things for granted and ate what was served to them. Times were tough.

Dad moved to Sudbury at the age of nineteen, and started to work for the mining giant, INCO. During the strikes, he'd find work for the Canadian National Railroad (CN), and would have to leave for a week or two at a time. He was always a hard worker, and developed many skills.

I was Dad's sidekick when I was little. I helped him to build the garage and dig out the pool. I remember being mortified when he buried a frog in the cinder block footings of the garage with cement! On our trip to Florida, he let me ride on his shoulders and walk all over his back with my sandy feet. In the winter, he'd give me rides in the snow float, on the snowmobile and he took me with him to set up snares for rabbits.

My Dad could build anything, fix anything, and was stronger than anyone I knew. He sometimes would come home after a late shift, with a Cortina meatball submarine sandwich. I would sneak out of bed, and beg him for a bite. He enjoyed watching hockey, and would shout out "He Scores!", at which point, I would pitter patter down the hall from my bedroom to the living room, to tell him he was being too loud.

He wasn't a heavy drinker, but he would enjoy the occasional Blue light beer or Rye and coke. I never liked the smell of rye whiskey. Both of my parents smoked cigarettes when they were first married, but only Dad was able to quit before I was born. Mom stopped later, I was four or five then, and I remember telling Nan, "Nanny, Mommy is smoking again!", as I sat on the designated chair below the flesh coloured rotary dial telephone that hung on the interior brick wall. I liked to curl the coiled cord around my little fingers.

We had a nice bungalow on Percy Street in Flake Subdivision in the little town of Val Caron. This was just to the North of Sudbury and formed part of "The Valley". Grown-ups jested that our group of five friends were the "Valley Girls". We didn't understand the reference that was from a show before our time.

I loved my home on Percy Street, in Val Caron. We had a nice big yard, sculpted cedar trees (from Manitoulin island), a garden, a big deck, and an inground swimming pool. I grew up in the late 1970's and 1980's, so we had the green and gold carpeting, the white sheer curtains, crystals hanging from the lamps on the coffee tables and a five-foot-long turntable in a beautiful brown wooden box with legs. We couldn't play in the living room when there were records playing, as they would skip. I had "Disco Duck", and liked playing it on 45-speed which was intended for the smaller records. It made the voices on the larger albums sound like "The Chipmunks". I also really liked an album with a variety of more current grown up songs like: "Born to be alive", "Abracadabra" and "Celebration". I felt pretty rebellious listening to Abracadabra and singing along to the verse: "black panties with an angel's face". Most people had a living room for show, only. Sometimes the furniture or appliances were still covered in protective plastic, and the vacuum treads in the carpet had to be just so. But, we were allowed to sit and play in our living room.

Dad always wanted to listen to Country Western music or Harry Hibbs, which made him want to grab one of us to do the Polka. We called it "Newfie music", as we assumed it was what he was accustomed to from when he lived in Newfoundland. Mom and

Dad were really good dancers. They knew how to jive, and I heard they were pretty good at it. They only went on dancing dates once in a while. My parents didn't entertain very much. In fact, my parents didn't have many friends. Our house was always clean, though, and they took good care of us. I spent lots of my time practicing my somersaults and back bends, and hanging upside down on my monkey bars, with my two blonde pigtails hanging down. Often the kids from the neighbourhood would watch from the fence in hopes of being invited to come for a swim.

Mom was born in Shawville, Quebec, and lived in Starks Corners. Her Dad was a dental assistant during the war, and he didn't get to meet his first born, Dianne, until she was a toddler. After the war, he worked for the Canadian National Railway in Ottawa and came home on weekends. When Mom turned six, they moved to Ottawa. They didn't speak French. My Grandfather was of German descent. My Grandmother had English on her side. Dianne became a nurse, married Rodney, and they settled in Ottawa.

Mom and her parents moved to Sudbury while she was still in high school. Before they moved, my Mom, my Grandfather and Mom's Uncle Fred, were in a car accident. My Grandfather thought my Mom was pinned beneath the car. With the miraculous strength that comes from this fear, he lifted the car to save her. But, she was not pinned beneath and was fine, but he hurt himself in the process. My Grandfather had to change jobs, due to his injuries, and decided to move the family to Sudbury.

My Grandparents moved into an apartment building on Cypress Street in downtown Sudbury. This was the very same building where Dad rented a room from a wonderful lady by the name of Polly Wall. That's where Mom and Dad first met. They fell in love sometime after her Prom. She invited him to her Prom but made other plans, as he was going to be in Newfoundland. He came back to surprise her and take her to the party, but she wasn't around. Dad loved to surprise people, and rarely gave advanced notice before he showed up. They married in 1968. When they announced their engagement to my

Grandparents, Nan said something to Dad that would stain their relationship and stay with him a long time: "I don't think you're good enough for my daughter....". It's amazing how powerful some words can be. After their first year married, my Grandfather succumbed to a brain tumour. Mom thought that the stress that brought on this tumour might have been due to the car accident. I wish I could have met him. I made him a poem during a poetry assignment in Grade Nine, based on the stories that Mom would tell:

My Grandfather

He wrote her every day, of the three years that he was away.
Their child kissed his picture each night, the
one sitting next to her bedside light.
Then on the day he finally returned, their child
knew him only by what she had learned.
Come for a walk said he to his child and she looked
insecurely at her Mother, who smiled.
Soon into the world they brought another.
A dark-haired girl, unlike the other.
He found a lucky penny one day. It's sad that he framed it, in a way.
As a year later, with cancer he died.
That lucky penny, had lied.

Dad said that Mom took after her father, in many ways. He was calm, kind, and a good listener. Mom was always the one who would listen to me, and always knew how to make me feel better. We went on two trips, as a convoy with some of our neighbours to Florida when I was three and four. We stayed at a campground in Kissimmee, near Disney world. While there, I fell off the dome shaped monkey bars at the park and landed straddling a bar. How do you treat a bruised 'petunia'? Mom knew just what to do. She sat me on a lawn chair, placed my feet in a square plastic basin of warm water and gave me a can of Coca-cola (Coke), a soft drink.

I'll never forget riding on the back of Mom's bicycle in the child seat. I must have been small, but remember the wind through my hair, the bumps in the road and fun hills on the path beside Main Street where Flake Subdivision joined up with the field beside Confederation high school. I always felt safe, and loved.

Mom and I grew to have more of a friendship, she spoke to me as an adult, rather than a child and she would always be game for cross country skiing or bike rides, music concerts and walks to talk about things. Mom had hazel eyes and hair that she would dye regularly. It was usually below her shoulders and layered, and always looked a little orange.

She always dressed up for her job as a "Credit Control Officer" at the Bank of Montreal, and while at home, you would always find Mom donning a neck to ankle housecoat that zipped down the front length. It was similar to the action of a superhero, as they shed their outer layer to uncover their uniform. Mom was my superhero. We always had to give her time before talking to her when she first walked in the door, likely from all of the credit control saves she had to make that day. After working all day, she needed time to unwind.

Dad was a really good cook. He would have Mom's supper ready on a plate, kept warm and covered with melted plastic wrap. She always had the silliest sayings, too. These likely were inherited from Nan. Sometimes it was difficult to understand them in conversation when they'd say things like: "If ifs and ands were pots and pans, there wouldn't be any tinkers!", "Don't throw the baby out with the bathwater", "Can't make a silk purse out of a sow's ear", or "Knee high to a grasshopper" "Heavens to Mugatroyd!" I find myself reciting some once in a while, and laugh at myself when I catch them coming out.

I was really a people pleaser, so I had no trouble following the rules, of which there were many. Their rules made me understand what was expected of me, how to be a good person, and how to make my parents happy. I loved to make them proud of me. I loved my Nan, too. Nan loved to dance and play bridge and she came over most Sunday afternoons for dinner with us. She was a fancy dresser, and usually had polyester pant suits in all colours. Red, yellow, baby blue, and a pretty button up blouse to match, accessorized with clip on earrings. I was always surprised that Mom let her wear her shoes in the house.

Nan didn't understand why I was so private. It was really humiliating to me once when I had a fever and she had come over to take care of me. She made me strip and she rubbed 70% isopropyl alcohol on me to cool me off. It was uncomfortable to be naked, even if it was in front of my Nan, and the alcohol was very cold! Sometimes I got to sleep over at her place. Nan always had her housecoat that would reach the floor and zip almost all the way up in front, just like Mom's. She had such nice teacups and china, and she always had these little creamy candy mints in a crystal candy jar. Sometimes she'd put pin curls in my hair before bed to make my hair curly, and she had a big bag attached to a canister that she would seal over my hair, and this was supposed to help dry my hair. It didn't blow very hard, and I found it quite boring to sit through.

The next day, when the pin curls came out, my hair was quite contrary and full of misguided curls. It took much self-control not to cry in front of Nan, when I disliked my hairdo and I was eager to wash it out when I got home. Nan had a green toilet and green bathtub, and the bathroom always smelled of roses and Chanel No. 5, or Chantilly. Funny how a smell or a certain melody, (Nan loved to listen to Zamfir), still brings me back to Rumball Terrace. That was the name of the apartment building where Nan lived. She taught me to knit, and some basic crochet. She made me an Icelandic sweater, where there were multiple colours around the neckline, and a solid colour for the remaining body and arms. Unfortunately, the armpit holes were so tight, that I had to keep my arms straight out to my sides, in order to keep the neck where it was supposed to sit. Otherwise, the chest portion would buckle and poke out awkwardly. I only wore it when she visited.

Nan always said she could write a book. She had nice stories about when Mom and Aunt Dianne were young, and when my Grandfather would get cold feet, she'd tell him "change your socks, Herbert". She recorded some of these stories on a mini cassette recorder, as I told her that I would write her story.

My parents lost a baby after me, and I remember that cold, dark night, being carried from my bed to my neighbours' house, by Mr. Whitmore. They lived around the corner on Clairview Avenue. Dad rushed Mom to the hospital. I was about three or four at the time, so I did not understand what was going on. I don't think that I even knew that Mom was with child. I was very comfortable with the Whitmore's, as they babysat me on occasion and I liked to play with their daughter, Jennifer. She was a year older than me. I didn't feel traumatized whatsoever by that night. It was kind of fun being carried outside in my pajamas! Afterwards, Mom and Dad figured that they should adopt, so they could have a boy and a girl.

When they were approved to adopt, Mom found out she was pregnant for my sister, Melanie. So, they decided to go ahead with adopting a boy, but had to wait until Mel was two before proceeding. Melanie Jill, she had to have a "J" in her name because Mom, Dad and I all had names that started with a "J". Melanie was my new doll. She was chubby, with huge blue eyes and curly blonde locks. Her giggles were quite contagious. I'm not sure Mom was aware, when I would place her in my hard plastic, pink doll carriage. I would then carry her to the basement, to the playroom, down twelve or so stairs, and I was about six or seven years old. It's amazing that I never dropped her! As she grew, she was my shadow. Mom even dressed us in the same dresses once. I was not impressed, but she was giddy with excitement! Her laughter was particularly contagious. She would get everyone laughing when something tickled her funny bone, she was adorable, and knew it.

Mel was two, and I was eight years old when we adopted BJ (BJ was six years old). The first time we visited with him in Peterborough, Ontario, we were tenting. He had a rough beginning. He was taken from his grandparents when he was very young, and bounced around until the police, Children's Aid Society (CAS) and police dogs found him one day, when his uncle had him running through the forests, through rivers to hide their scent. It was a rough beginning, for him. The idea of a "brother" was a novelty to me, and I wanted to spend each minute with him, but wasn't comfortable changing in the same tent, so I averted my eyes when he got his swimsuit on. We were all very excited to have him join the family. He wasn't too sure about his new surroundings, and seemed a little distrustful right from the start.

Mel and I had to share a bedroom, and it was a yellow Holly Hobby motif with yellow and white frilly twin bed sets. BJ, was a different species altogether. He had a dark brown hair with a bit of a wave, and a few freckles. He had blue eyes, high cheekbones and a square jaw. He was a good-looking kid, but had a hard time fitting in.

We had some good times, though. I loved being able to play with his toys, and having a sibling that was close to my age. He had the Millennium Falcon and Star Wars action figures. His bedroom walls were covered with Marvel wallpaper, with The Flash, Shazam, and the Hulk, and he was pretty good at drawing them too! Nan crocheted him a multi-shaded blue afghan, as his bedspread. He had a room all to himself. BJ and I enjoyed Lawn Darts, bike rides, frisbee and playing baseball and football with the neighbourhood kids. We even did some play fighting and I accidentally gave him a nosebleed. I realized then, that he could get really angry.

We went on family trips to Newfoundland every four years. The last time, BJ was ten and I was twelve. Our two male cousins Scott and Timothy, also twelve, invited us to go swimming at the salmon hole. I had one of those bathing suits that crossed in the back and tied at the center of my back. My teeny breasts were about the size of shelled peanuts. Once at the salmon hole, Scott grabbed hold of the bow that held my bathing suit in place and threatened to pull if I didn't say which of the two of them, I liked better. I was so angry with BJ for not coming to my rescue, so I told them I liked "Scott" better (he did have my bathing suit in hand). They even called me our Grandparents' place later to ask me, in a muffled voice, if I had "The Big P?". I had no idea what they were talking about. I was so naive that once I had started my period, a grade eight boy hugged me from behind during recess, and I thought I might be pregnant! Parents were not so open with their kids then, and anatomy was taught in health class in high school.

BJ was in the Core English Program at Valley View Public School. He did pretty well in school, but his temper seemed to be his biggest hang up. I had to babysit both my brother and sister often, especially after school. There was one weekend, that Mom and Dad had an overnight, and I had to hold the fort. It was on my watch, that BJ went to play street hockey down the street about five houses down the road, in front of our friends' house. During the game, he was hit by a car. He suffered a broken leg and the driver's insurance paid him $13 000 for it, which our parents put aside for him.

As BJ aged, he became more defiant and aggressive towards Mom. She never really had a soft spot for him, and I'm sure he sensed it. Dad would get so mad at him. It used to scare me, and I would take Mel aside and try to comfort her. I remember praying that one day, it would just be me and Mel.

Mom and Dad slowly grew apart, and then started filling my ears with their separate troubles. I would escape to my downstairs bedroom, that Dad built for me so that I no longer had to share with Mel. It was a pretty pink room, with my little tiled vanity with a sink in the corner, and posters of Christopher Reeve in his Superman costume, and Bo Duke (John Schneider) and Luke Duke (Tom Wopat) from the Dukes of Hazards TV series. My bedspread was a comforter with light gray and light pink. I loved spending time in my room. While there I would knit, organize my things, listen to Michael Jackson, and then Def Leppard music on my bright yellow walk-man or my ghetto-blaster and write in my diary.

Most kids were into drinking and sex, way before I had even had my first kiss...at 16...It used to drive me crazy when Dad would say "Sweet Sixteen and never been kissed!". Only because it was true! The summer that I turned sixteen, I had my first kiss. It was with our parents' friends' son, Rodney L. I did not know what to expect, but found it most addictive. He wasn't very creative, he would just stick his tongue out and in again, and repeated that motion for the duration. I had nothing with which to compare, and found it fascinating. He broke up with me, because I wouldn't go any further with him. That year, we moved out of the Valley to New Sudbury, near my high school.

I went to Lasalle Secondary School, as Confederation Secondary did not yet offer French Immersion. We moved to a blue side split house on Yarmouth avenue, and we only stayed there for a year and then moved to Springdale. The Springdale house was a nice, brown, back split house, with three bedrooms upstairs and one downstairs. It was a nice open concept, where you could see into the family room through the banister from the living room. It would take me about twenty minutes to walk to school from there. It was a nice neighbourhood, but the train track behind it took some getting used to. I missed walking home from school with my crush Eddie, when I lived on Yarmouth. I once took a picture of him walking by our house on his way home, while listening to Lionel Ritchie's song "Hello" (is it me you're looking for?).

I always liked telling my friends that BJ ran away with the circus, because it was almost true. He had been sent to a group home at around thirteen or fourteen years of age, because he was violent with Mom and Nan. Then at sixteen he got a job with the Midway, which was like a traveling circus, with games and rides. He went with the Midway, with his $13 000, in hopes to find his real parents. We didn't hear from him much after that. Enough to know that he found his parents, and nurtured a big chip on his shoulder, and he blamed his biological Mother of manipulating him out of his insurance money.

When we started Grade nine, we met this city girl named "Sharon". She had brown eyes and big, curly light brown hair from a spiral perm. Her hair didn't move when she moved her head due to the amount of hairspray we used then. Her parents were Caucasian, but they were both from Trinidad. She had this secret to meeting boys. She would stare at a cute boy, until she could get him to look her way. She would keep staring at him, until they made conversation. She also taught us to do repetitious lifts to our tippee-toes to make our calves look more muscular and hence more appealing to boys.

We tried her eye contact technique at the local hockey arena during the Sudbury Wolves game, because there were always lots of boys there. Sharon often had parties when her parents were away. The parties always involved booze. I managed to stay away from alcohol until a party at Shelley's boyfriend's house, when I was seventeen. I had about seven Long Island iced teas. They tasted so good, and I had no idea how much one should drink. I blacked out behind a chair in the living room at this strange house. I felt sick and could not move.

I once tried to have a party at my house, but both of my parents were home. There was no alcohol, so the 20-30 that showed up left shortly after we finished watching "The Little Mermaid" movie. I was pretty embarrassed at how lame my party was.

In order to get fit, I tried jogging. Dad used to laugh at the way I ran, so I would only go out for a jog in the evenings, when it was dark. I just couldn't get over the taste of blood in the back of my throat, and the feel of water on the lungs. This body was not built to run.

My first non-babysitting job was at Sweet and Saucey (Pizza and Donut Shop), which is where I met Wayne and then Alejandro. Wayne was a little slimy and gave me Mononucleosis. I didn't like that he smoked and always smelled of cherry halls. I broke up with him, and then fell for Alejandro. I was sixteen, and he was nineteen. He was a dark, mysterious, older man from Uruguay. This should have been the first sign! (U-R-Gay). His accent was so appealing, and he was so friendly. We started dating, and he would say such nice things then translate them, like "estoy enamorando" ('I am in love'), and "yo quiero" ('I want you'), and I couldn't wait until the next kiss. It seemed he had only rations to spare, for good behaviour.

Alejandro encouraged me to get out of my pretty pink room and learn what was going on in the outside world. He also encouraged me to get out and do some volunteering. He had a lot of opinions about everything. I would usually take the Sudbury Transit to go and visit him. He stayed with his aunt and uncle who had a home behind Gloria's restaurant, off Martindale Road. It was a long bus ride, having to take two busses to get there. He once took me to a friend Richard's for a party. The house was on a lake, and I didn't know that I was supposed to bring a bathing suit. His friend's Mom had a spare bikini for me, the colour was faded from this taupe material with tired looking flowers. The material was overstretched, and not flattering in the least! I didn't feel I had any choice. I was not skinny, I was not fat, but I was not toned either...to make it worse, Alejandro never once looked at me.

He was my boyfriend for almost two years, until one night I was out with him until 3:00 am, talking. He tried to get it across to me that his friend Richard, was moving away and it made him very sad. It made him very, very sad. "Ohhhh! You mean you're gay?" Was it the bikini?

I think that hurt more than leaving me for another girl! He was my very awkward first love, and I lost my virginity to him, though he was so small and not very interested, that it really shouldn't have counted. He tried to explain about the different 'shades of gay', but I was heartbroken. He was still confused however, and I thought I still had a chance, since he thought he would want to be with a person because of who they are and not their gender. He moved here to explore that side of his nature. Dad waited up for me that night, and the only thing he said when I walked in the door, was

"That's the last time, I lose sleep over some Spaniard!" My relationship with Alejandro started to evolve into more of a friendship, as I dealt with not being "the one", and felt I still needed him in my life in any way possible. Here is a poem that he inspired me to write, I had written it in Calligraphy and framed it for him as a gift.

Thinking of You

A simple thought rules this hand,
to express what I see, here where I stand.
Not a figure but a feeling follows me here.
Like a welcoming smile or a kindly ear.
Happily and most gratefully I stand and look
and see with new prospect this babbling brook.
It was once only water, but now I can see an image projected back at me.
Familiar, yet not, it is me, a new.
In the eyes I can see, I am thinking of you.
You are my strength, my faith, my friend.
You've given me peace, to you, peace I send.

He loved it, and at first, he suspected that I copied it but then realized that it was my own work. At this point, I felt I had closure from my Chapter with Alejandro. Perhaps, I relied upon him, to distract me from Mom and Dad's issues. I watched a presentation with him by a John Brad (Bradshaw) talking about the wounded inner child. This inspired me to write a poem, and letters in my non-dominant hand. I wrote a letter to each of my parents, and my sister...as if it was the child in me speaking to them. It was pretty good therapy, and it still brings a tear to my eye.

Close to my heart

Child so sweet, so kind, so fragile.
Where have you gone? I can see you not.
A sweet remembrance, a moment, a while
Is all I can sense, like deep-rooted knot.
I close my eyes and travel through time
Seeing images so familiar of what once I called home.
A small child standing alone with tears that were mine
Seems lost and abandoned to aimlessly roam.
I try to approach this beautiful one
Feeling a pull towards her innocent face.
She looks at me, needs not to atone
And runs into my arms to embrace
I then hold her near, close to my heart
The smile of contentment lightens her face
This is what I need to go on with my life
My hurt inner child healed from her outer strife.

To: Mommy

I love you very much. You have always been there for me, and have given me strength when I haven't felt too good. You have always believed in me and were the first to believe me when I said I was telling the truth. I wish I could hold you in my arms like you used to do with me, and give your forehead a kiss and tell you that everything is going to be O.K. but we don't do those things anymore, when did we start hiding our feelings? Maybe, it was when I started listening to your unhappiness and didn't think that a kiss would make it better anymore. I'm sorry Mommy, I just want you to know that I will always love you and want you to be happy. Do what you know will bring you the most happiness. I love you Mommy! Love Jan xoxo

To: Daddy

I love you up to the sky and back down again! Daddy, member when you used to sing to, "You are my sunshine, my only sunshine, you make me happy when skies are gray, you'll never know dear how much I love you please don't take my sunshine away...?" I loved that! I remember feeling safe and happy. We were happy then, weren't we? I loved when you would take us camping and fishing. I loved when you'd put the worm on my hook for me. You were so good at it! I loved when you played ball with me, and frisbee. But we don't do any of that anymore because we are always too busy and you would rather play with your friends. Daddy, how do we show you we love you when you're not here and don't want to play with us anymore? I sure would like us all to go camping again! Daddy, I don't like seeing you sad and I don't like what you tell me when you're sad so stop being sad cause we need you! I love you Daddy xoxo

To: Mel

I love you Mel. I love your name because I got to help pick it. I love you because you're my baby sister and you're fun to feed with the bottle. Your head was too heavy on my arm, but that was O.K., 'cause Mommy put a pillow there to help me. I remember looking at you and your big, blue eyes, I wondered what you would be like when you grew up. You turned even better that I thought! I'm proud of you. I love you, Mel (Be happy!) Love Jan xoxo"

My parents decided to see a marriage counsellor. It seemed that Mom was on the verge of a nervous breakdown and Dad had been taking the blame for everything. He moved his things downstairs into the spare bedroom, and Mel wasn't too happy about that, because that's where she played with the Nintendo gaming console.

I got a job at a local cocktail bar, called "Zap's" and I started dating a bouncer, named J.P.(Jean-Paul). I warned him that I was probably on the rebound. He was a football player, not very smart, not very cute, but he was sweet and muscular, and adored me. He called me "gorgeous" all of the time, wrote me two poems, and called me every day. He would always play his Midnight Oil cassette when we were in the car. He would get very jealous when other guys would flirt with me at the bar, and wanted to protect me. He helped to repair my ego. He gave me a big hug and asked me to never let him go. He told me he loved me after one month. He was my Prom date, and we lasted two months.

I moved on from J.P., to this new waiter, named Dan. Dan was tall, had a nice build, brown eyes and a few freckles. He was suave and funny, and very likeable. I was smitten with him. After a couple of afterhours parties with the crew from Zap's, we had our first kiss. He stayed with his sister Cindy and her husband and two boys near Adanac ski hill in New Sudbury. He had a little corner in their basement for all of his worldly belongings, and his mattress. I loved spending time with him, and thought the sex was pretty great. I think it was because he was great at cuddling. But, I had yet to experience an orgasm. The song "Everything I do", from the Robin Hood movie soundtrack, was our song.

It was so uncomfortable around the house those days when both Mom and Dad were at home. The living room was Mom's space, and the family room was Dad's. They lived awkwardly separate lives for a while, until one day I talked to them together and said that I couldn't handle them talking to me anymore about each other, that they should just get a divorce. I don't think I've ever been able to forget that moment. They separated soon thereafter. It didn't help that neighbours and my Nan had both filled Mom's ears with seeds of doubt about her marriage. BJ really had brought out the worst in both of them, but I wished I hadn't been the one to say it. I felt ultimately responsible for their ensuing unhappiness and regret.

I had a great upbringing, and never once felt unloved. However, I did feel the sadness of my parents, the loss of my brother, and the need to protect my sister. I felt like I needed to help them all. Maybe this was my role. To help others? But making my parents' divorce wasn't giving them a happy ending. I felt resentful to my brother for making them so distant and mad at myself for telling them. I was also resentful, that I turned Alejandro gay, after almost two years.

I decided that I would not end up like my parents. I would learn from their mistakes, and to me that meant to live on my own. Mom never lived on her own before getting married. Once I graduated, I would go to a University out of town. I had to get away from Sudbury, and all of the sadness that I felt. Dan thought of following me out of town, but Dad said that he would not support me, if I was going to be shacked up with someone. Dan stayed in Sudbury, and we tried the long-distance relationship. Mom and Dad sold the house, and found apartments, and Mel moved in with Mom. I was accepted into the Bachelor of Science Program, Majoring in Biology at Queen's University, in Kingston, Ontario.

CHAPTER TWO

Just a Friend

Queen's University - Oil thigh na Banrighinn, a' Banrighinn gu brath!

There I was, alone, in a new city. It was thrilling and frightening all at the same time! It was comforting that I already knew who my roommate at the Victoria Hall Co-Ed Residence was, because Ellen and I requested to share a room when we found out we were both attending Queen's University in Kingston, Ontario. She was taking Mechanical Engineering and I was taking a Biology Major. I was going to be a "Dental Surgeon, a Poet and a Calligraphy Artist". Dentistry was a very competitive program, that needed high undergrad marks as a prerequisite.

Ellen was a tall, thin, fair girl with big blue eyes and a very big, smiley mouth. Her teeth were always showing as she had a permanent smile on her face. She was fun, and she had the comfort of two older brothers who were also attending Queen's, Matt and Ross. One was doing his masters, the other in his second or third year engineering which was great when we wanted to go and rent a movie or enjoy some home cooking that their Mom had sent.

During Frosh week, Ellen consented to be sprayed purple with the other Engineer Frosh and chopped off part of her hair at the back, not quite willing to get the popular Mohawk. Once purpled, students were not permitted in residence, so she had to stay at her brother's house, until the purple paint wore off. Ellen never seemed to get overly stressed out about anything. She didn't seem to be a very serious student and I didn't think she'd make it in the difficult engineering program. She finished Engineering, and got her Masters.

I found out, in short order, that my own 83% average was very hard to maintain in University. Not only did I miss home, but found the two hundred plus class size to be overwhelming. I felt like I was just a tiny little ant in an ant farm, and shriveled down in my seat. I felt invisible. I should have known by the school's anthem, the Gaelic "Oil thigh na Banrighinn a'Banrighinn gu brath." that language was not a significant barrier, for employment. The Professors were very smart and published, but I didn't think that English proficiency was a prerequisite. My Chemistry Professor (Prof) was Russian, my Calculus Prof spoke Cantonese or Mandarin, and I wished I could have blamed my Physics Prof of something, because I just could not grasp the subject, and failed. My first failure, ever. It was humbling. I was not going to get accepted into Dentistry.

I went to talk to a school counselor, named Gisèle. She had me divulge my entire last twelve months, and she had me convinced that Alejandro had forced himself upon me. I was so impressionable back then, and looking back, remembered how when I told Alejandro that I had moved on and found someone else, he asked if I was trying to hurt him. He wanted to show me, that he could love me like that, and gave me a very "aggressive" kiss. I was not interested in getting this attention from him, and was able to stop him, but Gisèle had me convinced that I was a victim.

I took a bus to Sudbury to spend the weekend with Dan, and I didn't tell my parents. I called Mom from his place, so that she wouldn't call me in Kingston and find out that I was actually in Sudbury. They didn't have the call display function yet, to find out what number was calling. I talked to Mom about the weather, and felt incredibly guilty. I'm not usually one to lie, and am not very good at it. I enjoyed the break just the same. I really loved this guy. I was a little concerned that he wasn't getting anywhere in life, and I was worried he would turn out to be an alcoholic, like his Dad.

A few months later, Dan came to visit me. He got a ride to Kingston with my ex-boyfriend, J.P., to spend a few days in residence with me. J.P.'s friend Chris was in the engineering program. Apparently, Chris had been the author of the poem that I thought J.P. had written to me. Ellen stayed at her brothers to give us privacy. As soon as he arrived, he broke up with me. He found that this long-distance relationship was too difficult. Since he was to stay for a couple of days, I told him he could stay with me anyway, and make it our farewell party. It was bittersweet. I was heartbroken.

I got my tonsils out that year, and Mom couldn't even be there when I awoke in the Hotel Dieu hospital and vomited through my new stitches. Alone. I lost ten pounds in one week, and then Ellen forced me to get up and get moving. With a little purpose and more food, I came back to life. I missed home. Every night, I still said a prayer before falling asleep. I had started following my "Now I lay me down to sleep…" Prayer with the Serenity prayer, that was inscribed on a little wooden plaque that used to belong to my Maternal Grandfather:

"God grant me the Serenity to accept the things
I cannot change. The courage to change the things
I can and the wisdom to know the difference."
Author Unknown

I gave Queen's another year, and even tried my best to get over my homesickness, by stepping out of my comfort zone, and staying in Kingston for the summer. I worked at Megalo's as a "Soda-bartender", preparing ice cream desserts, and special coffees. It was here that I discovered an appreciation for Jazz and Blues. On Sunday nights, downstairs from Megalos at "Papa Louis bar", they had blues night, with a live blues band. The atmosphere was dim, and smoky, because that was okay then. The bartender was a student from France, named Brett. He had a beautiful French accent, not like Franglais or Québécois French. Bar comers would also get up and start singing. It was moving. My new favourite song, was "Moondance". I had no rules, but the ones I chose to keep.

We had a three-bedroom apartment near the corner of Princess and Division, next to the gay bar "Robert's Club Vogue". It was only a ten-minute walk to work, and to the University. My new roommates, Becky (from Midland and also in Biology) and Marcia (Commerce student, from Bolivia) went home for the summer. I saw a few guys that year, to try to fill some holes in my heart. I also didn't think Mom had dated enough, and I was determined not to make the same mistake.

A friend of my boss' at Megalo's, by the name of Chris, visited my soda bar a few times. He was flattering and interesting. He walked me back to my apartment, and I invited him in. He said that he was separated. I immediately regretted consenting to his visit and hated myself for being such an easy target. He had blond curly hair and no freckles or hair on the trunk of his body, and the smoothest skin. I noticed these things. I preferred a man with hair on his chest. He wore my red lingerie underwear, but I didn't find that appealing... All I needed was a hug. I was starving for affection. I missed Dan.

Then there was Sam. He had dark, curly hair and deep blue eyes and a sheepish, but adorable smile. He had a lean, but muscular build, and looked like a thin baseball player. We dated for a few months. I respected him for his abstinence as he confessed to having genital warts that he didn't want to share. Apparently, his close male friend also had them and I wondered how *close* they actually were.

My room was no longer pink, but a grayish-white, and I had a floral comforter from back home. I took the odd-shaped bedroom, above a stairway, off the kitchen and living room. There was a ledge, that fit a single mattress, with no box spring, and I had a little step ladder to get up to it. Valerie, my new friend from work had a sewing machine, and helped me make coordinating toss pillows in pinks and greens, which made it comfier. I had a pillowcase for a window covering, as it was at the foot of my bed and the apartment was only one level up from street level and there were used drug related needles and paraphernalia on the ground below.

Sometimes, we'd frequent the "Chinese Laundry" cafe for coffee and cheesecake, or the Library, or on the weekends we'd go to "Dollar Bills", or some other bar, to dance. I would try Sharon's eye contact technique. We were at Dollar Bills once when Actor Dan Akroyd showed up with a couple of bodyguards. He put his arm around Ellen, my first-year roommate, and said in jest that he'd "take this one home!".

Becky and Marcia were good students and liked to have fun on the weekends. We tried learning Spanish so we made our grocery list in Spanish and learned some bad words from Marcia. We called each other 'affectionate' names like "Putita", from a not so nice "Puta", which meant "Whore", and adding "-ita" (little), was meant lovingly, "Little Whore". Marcia also had two brothers that were at Queen's, in the Engineering program. She started dating a friend of her older brother's, named Derek. Becky also had an adopted brother, but he was still in Midland. She had a long-term boyfriend back home that she was trying to get over, and would lament while listening to Sting's song "Fields of Gold".

We went to get professional pictures taken together with all kinds of props. These were my new sisters. We had dinner together some nights, and watched Golden Girls together, on the television we were renting, sitting on the old hide-away-bed couch that Becky's parents had provided. This was home away from home. They were very studious and seemed more successful than I at keeping their heads on straight and their marks up.

I tried getting a co-worker, Chandler, to tutor me in physics, but I gave up on trying to get it, and kissed him instead. He was really tall, with big ears. He was fit, and sweated profusely during sex. It was almost funny, when his forehead would drop onto me, stinging my eyes with his salty sweat. I would call him once in a while and we'd talk dirty to each other, to the point he just had to come for a visit. He never wanted a girlfriend, because he was just too busy. I wished he was Dan.

Ellen's brother, Ross, invited me to a semi-formal. I was hoping that he meant nothing more than to cheer me up, because I didn't want to hurt his feelings. I hated to say "no". I hated where I was heading, which was nowhere. I was in my second year of biology. I was just passing, and on probation.

During Christmas break, I went home for a three-week holiday. I got a ride back to Sudbury, after the December exams with Curtis. I met him a few months prior at Dollar Bill's when Ellen introduced her engineering friends. I had my eye on him until he showed an interest in Becky, and our friend TJ. When I found out that he was from Sudbury, I thought that would have been convenient and nice if he'd been interested in me. After the bar, TJ and Curtis saw each other for a few weeks, then it dwindled. I knew he was driving home, so I asked for a ride. I honestly, had no ulterior motives. In the car was Curtis, his friend Sean, and myself. We talked all the way home and shared funny stories and listened to music. Usually, I couldn't hear what they were saying in the front seat. By the end of the ride, I mentioned that I'd be going to Ralph's bar on Wednesday, three days later. I went to Ralph's, and stood in line with my small dress shoes in the middle of winter. Many of my high school friends were there and I joined the party, with drinking Singapore Slings and shooters to warm up my toes. Then, I saw a Queen's engineer jacket, it was Curtis in his baseball cap. So, I went over to say "Hi". We spent a couple of hours together, it must have been that long. Talking and dancing and then kissing... oops! As soon as we made to leave the bar, some guy, under the influence, pushed Curtis from behind knocking me out of the way. He gave Curtis a black eye, then realized he had the wrong Queen's engineer and asked Curtis to hit him back. Curtis kept his cool and shook his hand instead. I thought, this was a decent guy. By then, my taxi came and he asked for my phone number, before I left. He didn't write it down, so I didn't think he would remember it, and I was right. He didn't know my last name and I didn't know his. Dad drove me back to Kingston. When giving Dad directions to the University, I saw a Queen's engineer jacket, I was pointing it out to my Dad and I realized that it was Curtis, so Dad honked and I waved, he waved back and called me two hours later, once Dad had left.

He apologized and told me how he tried finding my last name. He was worried that I'd think he was an asshole. He asked me if I wanted to go out with him and his friends the next night. He called me again at two in the morning and we talked for a bit. I liked this guy and would like to see more of him, but I was worried about what TJ would think. I thought I was becoming selfish because I didn't stop the kissing, and I didn't say no to seeing him. He stopped by the next day because he said he wanted some of the macaroni-tuna salad that I was making. It was sort of awkward at first then he said "You're shy, aren't you?", which appeared to open the door and we had some safe fun. It was so nice to be held again and kissed. TJ called while he was over, and we made plans to get together the next day.

During my visit with TJ, we talked about her and Curtis and I asked her if she would mind if I went out with him. She said she didn't mind, but I told her, that if she thought it would hinder our friendship, that I wouldn't see him. She said it wasn't her place to say no, and that she would be a little bothered by seeing him with anyone else. Before he left, we agreed to see each other casually, as he was not interested in anything more. He never called again.

I was set up on a date with a man named Theo. He was of Greek descent, as were many business owners in Kingston. He lived in the basement of his parents' house and was very demanding for attention. He was opinionated too. He told me I should start trimming my nose hairs. I also tried trimming my pubic hair, but in doing so, amputated a portion of my clitoris.

Theo also taught me that "bigger is definitely not better", as he had a penis that could have served double duty as a kickstand. It was the scariest thing I had ever seen. It was not a pleasant experience, and I was scared of it. Sex felt like there was an aggressive baby that desperately wanted back in the womb. He was pretty full of himself, with his big, shiny red sports car, and broke it off with me when I couldn't spend more time with him during exams.

Becky played "Happy Birthday" for me on her kazoo. It was my twenty-first birthday, in May. I had a Kahlua and milk (Brown Cow) drink to celebrate. I thought my twenty-first birthday was going to be the most depressing birthdays ever. How did Mom marry at twenty-one? Becky came home from work for lunch, and we ordered McDonald's (they delivered!), and she gave me a CD "The Spin Doctors". We were planning to go out to the "Cocomo's" bar that night with my friend Val, from work. Becky and I started drinking at 6:30, and Becky's friend Jill came over.

We walked over to Val's to pick her up and Becky convinced me to bring my instamatic camera. As soon as Val opened her door, I took her picture and we walked into her living room. Three other people from work were there, and shouted in unison "Surprise!". I didn't notice the streamers and birthday signage until later. I even had an ice cream cake! I was so touched! A couple of others from work came and we all walked to Megalo's and everyone sang "Happy

Birthday" to me when I walked in. We went to the Cocomo's and a few more joined us. It was nice to know that people cared enough to do this for me.

I was listening to one of the cassette tapes, that Nan recorded, and she inspired me when she said that, "We're never given a job we can't handle".

I made it through the second year, but Kingston was not where I wanted continue my journey. I was still struggling and worried about Mom, who was having a lot of pain from her newly diagnosed ulcerative colitis, migraines and macular degeneration in the center of her left eye. Nan was in and out of hospital a couple of times, and her Alzheimer's was really advancing. I wanted to be there for them. Even my brother was back in Sudbury. Mom and Dad were getting along better now, as friends, and Mel was growing up. I was missing it all.

A few days before moving home, Val and I got tattooed, at "Express you tattoo". Mine was to represent my Kingston experience to remind me what I was really looking for. I chose a teddy bear, and chose to have it placed on my upper left butt cheek, just below the panty line. I was a little embarrassed when the tattoo artist pulled my pants down on the table, which was open to the store. To my relief, she promptly covered everything around her canvas. I was comforted that she took new needles from sealed packages for my tattoo. It felt like she was dragging a sharp knife to my flesh, for the duration. Just when I thought she was done, she said, "Now, we colour it in!". Owwwwweeeee! The outline hurt more than the colour, and I was relieved when it was all done! Val had her tattoo on her ankle. She didn't seem to find it as painful as I did.

Dad was scheduled to come pick me up on August 5, 1993, and bring me and my belongings home. I got Becky and Marcia a new roommate from France, to replace me through student services and sublet my share of the apartment. I took the rest of the year off, to figure out my next move.

Dad bought me a car, two weeks after I moved home. A cherry red, 1998 Plymouth Sundance. It had only 69,000 kilometers on the odometer. At first, I stayed at Dad's during the week because now that I was back and working at Zap's again as a waitress, I had late hours. I was saving to pay back $2000 of the $6000 that Dad spent on my car, and my car insurance was $600 per year. It was only $20 to fill the gas tank.

Mom had not been in the greatest of moods and I had a hard time being around to witness how Mel treated her then. So, I started staying at Dad's more permanently.

I told Dan that I was back. I intentionally went to Woolworth's to buy hair mousse (I didn't use mousse), but knew he was a Manager there. I was disappointed that he didn't have much of a reaction. We were completely over. I guess I needed that closure.

It was nice to be back. It was nice to be able to drive Mel to her job interview at Tim Horton's. She made me laugh when she heard she was hired and performed a little cheerleading dance praising the coffee shop.

Dad and I got along pretty well. We'd go out for lunch to Pizza Hut for their buffet, and he got me used to the special sauce at Swiss Chalet. Every bar was good on one night or another for different age groups. Dad's favourite was Chevies (pronounced 'Shevies'), and it was mostly 50-year-olds plus there. I wished I had learned the jive! I liked to join him, but it made him worry that people would think he was dating a younger woman.

Dad and I lived in his blue and white A-frame house, with an open living room and dining room, a kitchen around the bend and then his bedroom beyond that. Just before his room were the stairs that led up to my room. It was cute, decorated in blue except for his black and white kitchen. I had the whole upper level to myself with one side my bedroom, and the other, my study, with a sectional. Dad had to cut up the sectional and put it back together to get it upstairs. It was cozy. I'd listen to "What is love?" as I got ready for my nights out, at my brass make up table.

Dad had no trouble meeting women, and wasn't always home at night. This gave me a lot of freedom, except for one night when I was given the responsibility to lock up Zap's and arm the building. I locked my car and house keys in the building, at 2:00 in the morning. I couldn't drive my car home and had enough money for a cab there, but not much more, as tips were not generous. Dad's little blue house, was not far from downtown on Janet Street, off Van Horne. But Dad wasn't home and I couldn't get in. I didn't know the neighbours there, and I lit the barbecue in order to keep warm. The mosquitos and the chill were unrelenting, so it made for a long, restless night. I walked down the street to the phone booth in the morning to find Dad, but couldn't reach him. I'd never been so happy to see his Chevy Silverado! (I called it the 'Studmobile'). I think he was worried when he pulled up and saw me lying on the front porch.

I decided the following September to give Biology another run. I registered at Laurentian University in Sudbury. The Professors were very fluent in English, and Organic Chemistry actually made sense, as the Professor used his body to demonstrate in three dimensions how a compound rotates. He was awesome! The classes were smaller, which made a huge difference in my confidence. I met Bethany, a fellow student, who approached me to be her Lab partner. Bethany and I became good friends. We'd get together to do aerobics with "Gilad" on VHS, and she'd invite me over for dinner. Her mom was a fantastic cook and introduced me to some amazing flavours, and her father introduced me to some nasty smells. I didn't know feta farts could smell so bad!

My marks were much improved as was my self-confidence and I discovered late in the second part of the year, a love for Microbiology! "This is what I want to do!", I said, and asked Dave, my T.A. (Teacher's Assistant) what kind of jobs I would involve microbiology. I soon was enrolled for the following September, at Cambrian College for their Medical Laboratory Technologist Program. I would waste no more time in Biology. It wasn't training me for anything that would give me a job other than research or teaching, and neither of those interested me.

My life was taking a turn and finally it was in a positive direction. I dated a short man, named Tom, but we were at different stages and his friends always were his priority, so after two months, I ended it. At the bar, trying to forget about Tom, I saw my co-worker Matthew. He gave great hugs. He asked me to give him a chance, and we started dating. He was twenty-nine years old, eight years my senior. Dad did not approve, but he didn't know him, either. I tried not to let his opinions influence how I felt about Matthew, but they kind of did. One night, after playing cards with friends, Matthew asked me why I liked him. Funny, I was asking myself the same question. I know some of the things I didn't like, thanks to Dad, and was hard pressed to think of what I liked. I had always liked him, and thought he was a really nice person, but I was not "in love". I supposed I wasn't being fair to Matthew. I liked spending time with him, I liked the affection, but I didn't see a future for us as he seemed to. I couldn't believe, I was finally thinking that! I liked that he said he didn't want to sleep with me yet, and he said it takes him a long time learning to trust someone enough to sleep with them... No pressure. The longer we dated, the more unsure I became.

Alejandro was in town from school for a bit, and we had a phone conversation during which he revealed that he knew Matthew. In fact, he knew him a little *too* well. He hesitated, and then he suggested strongly "Jan, you don't want to go out with him!" I felt a huge lump swelling in the pit of my stomach, that climbed up and tightened my throat. "Is he...bisexual?", I asked, and he said "Yes!". My hands started shaking almost violently. How could this happen to me, twice? Alejandro told me some of the things he knew without any inch of doubt that Matthew had done. He used to call Alejandro at the hotel and tell him what he wanted to do to him...they had sex when Matthew was living with his fiancé. All I could see was red. As much as I was having my doubts about him, I still felt deceived and it brought up those same feelings of anger.

Immediately after hanging up the phone with Alejandro, I drove recklessly to Matthew's apartment. It was midnight and knocked until he woke up and answered the door. Normally, this would make me feel guilty but not this day. I looked at him as severely as I could. He was happy to see me. I couldn't speak. He used both hands to clear the sleep from his eyes and put on his glasses. Before he sat in his new recliner, I leaned on the couch and asked him if I had ever told him about my ex-boyfriend that turned homosexual. He said "Yeah". I said, "Did I ever tell you his name?". He began to look a little uncomfortable, as he said "No…". I told him it was "Alejandro" and proceeded to ask if he knew him. He said innocently "Why would I know him?". I said "Well he knows you and says you know him." He denied quite convincingly and said he must have him mixed up with somebody else. I asked him straight out if he was bisexual and told him what Alejandro had told me about him. He continued to deny it. I almost believed him, but didn't give up. I said, "I trust Alejandro with my life."

Matthew whispered, "What if it was true?". I said "If it was true, I'd feel very led on". Matthew regressed. Looked at me straight in the eye. Somebody else was sitting in front of me, this wasn't my old friend Matthew, anymore. "That was a long time ago." I thought my eyes were going to pop right out from the force of the air that I took in. He explained that it was something he'd put behind him, that he saw a psychiatrist and it's over. He didn't want to lose me, he's chosen the way he wants to live and will fight to keep it. What is it about me that attracts homosexuals?

I joined the Ladies' softball league, with my co-worker, Lee-Ann. We went to the YMCA together for aerobics classes. Lee-Ann and her and her boyfriend Rick were lots of fun, and I went over to visit often to play cards. I'd always wanted to belong to a team, but found it more humiliating than fun. I had a good arm, but couldn't catch the ball, or swing to hit it. I sucked. I felt that I was undercover, as I was known only as "Janice, friend of Lee-Ann". I didn't like the name, but thought once I got either better at playing or got to know the girls more, that I might correct them.

I was starting to get a little jealous of the time Dad had been devoting to his latest love interest. We were supposed to spend time together but 'Marilyn' called, and just as suddenly, he was gone. I liked sitting in my new comfy daybed with my pink smelly candles lit, listening to Sting, which was reminding me of Becky. I realized that I was where I wanted to be. I was finding my place here in Sudbury. I hoped that one day, I could find my soulmate, someone to worship the ground I walk on and I, his.

I went to Mingles bar one night, and one of the girls from softball introduced me to Ron, an insurance salesman. He was almost always dressed in a suit, and looked like a model in them! He was divorced and had two kids. My co-workers thought he was gay too, but I really liked him. He introduced me to Country music through Randy Travis', "You've been too gone, for too long…", and wow, he also introduced me to the orgasm! Helllllllooooo! One day he left a note on my car windshield while I was working, which read:

"I love being with the most beautiful, loving and caring girl in the world. Love Rotten Ronnie".

After four months, Tony from work, saw Rotten Ronnie making out with a short-haired brunette. I was so jealous, but I guess it really had ended two weeks prior, when he wanted to clarify his feelings to me and said. "I don't want to ever get married again, or have any more kids." But, I did. Dad always said: "Meet at a bar, lose to a bar!"

I was seriously getting tired of my luck. I loaded my five-Disk CD (Compact Disks) player, with instrumentals, 'The Phantom of the Opera soundtrack' and my favourite heart breaking medley, and had a good cry. I had one co-worker named "Eva". Eva worked as a cook at Zap's with me and she was a warm, sweet, a granola crunching kind of sort. One day she was waving her hands and arms all around me as I waited for my drink order at the bar. I asked "Eva, what are you doing?". She replied, "I'm just combing your aura!". "I didn't know it was tangled", I said with a doubtful half smile. Maybe she was right.

Since Nan had been diagnosed with Alzheimer's, her tape cassettes were not too informative anymore for the book we planned to write. There were recordings of her talking to a bird out the apartment window, and of a one-sided phone call with Polly. She was placed in a Senior's residence, then into a long-term care facility, called Extendicare. It was sad to see her disappear from her shell, but I was kind of glad I could be around more during this time. Nan passed away on March 4, 1995 at 11:30 pm. Mom was there when she took her last breath. Nan's ankles were really bothering her and she cringed every time the nurses tried to put her feet up on some pillows. Her face was so swollen. They said it was because her body was starting to shut down, starting with her kidneys. I couldn't see her eyes when she opened them, ever so briefly. She was in such a daze that when we tried talking to her, I couldn't tell if she knew we were there but I did know that she was in pain. She had breast cancer, that we opted not to treat, because her Alzheimer's had progressed so far. Her breathing was such an effort. They gave her morphine, and Mom told us we could go. I had Beth with me, because we had just worked out. I wished I'd been there alone and had stayed with Mom, as she passed away after I had left and only Mom was there. Nan did not want an open casket for the wake, and was cremated. We each put a rose beside her marble-like encasement and left. There were just our two families there, with Dianne and Rod, Chris (my cousin) and Diane (Chris' wife), Mom, Mel and I.

I had another talk with my Grandfather, like he could hear my thoughts. I found it kind of strange sending my thoughts to Nan, now. I wrote a couple of poems for her while I grieved.

Nan

Love began the struggle.
Joy followed with greater gifts. A tragic loss, a new beginning.
Resentment and tied hands.
Unheard words, her only means.
But hurt ensued and then helplessness.
Back and forth, in time she flew.
In and out of reality.
Within a few years she re-lived.
A lifetime of ups and downs.
Day by day and night by night.
Time lost its appeal.
Strange places, old but new.
faces unfamiliar
Her persistent heart reminding
That her job was filled.
Hoping...

Love you

Tea parties for two
Yellow coasters we knit
Challenges you gave me
When you knew I could
You believed in me
Supportive and loving
You are an important part of me
Now, and always Nan.
I love you!

In May of the same year, my brother, BJ appeared at the door. He had a chipped front tooth, and longish, misguided hair. His face looked so tired and weathered for a 21-year-old. My heart reached out to him. His stories compelled me to act more of a mother figure. I wanted so badly to help him out. He had just been moving from place to place, continually searching for his missing pieces, his identity. I told him that the only way to do that is to get a stable life for himself and just live it. Stop blaming others for where you are in life, and make some positive changes. My words seemed to have tempted him as we looked for an apartment for him, here in Sudbury. I even offered to have his tooth capped if he would just stay in Sudbury and make something for himself. But, he wasn't ready. His belongings were still in Chatham, and he didn't drive. I wanted to help him, I wanted him to know that Mel and I were still his sisters and were there for him. And just like that, he was gone again.

Zap's, the bar that I worked at became less of a cocktail bar, and more of a tele-theatre wagering hangout. I was getting sick of the gamblers, and found them to be ignorant, demanding and cheap. The tips were scarce. We'd see the same old gamblers each day, and wonder what kind of family life they could possibly have?

There were a few, however, that would come in that were really nice, with whom we befriended and partied with after hours. This was how I met Mark and John. Mark, would come in with his Dad sometimes and have a Blue Light or a Caesar Salad. He was very friendly, and a little on the heavy side. He had curly blackish brown hair and a moustache, and brownish-amber eyes. He had a kind face, and he looked like a teddy bear. Sometimes, he'd stop in with his friend John. John was a thin, athletic man, and was always smiling. He had a soft voice, blue eyes and a pointy nose.

I sat with Mark one day after my shift, and he was talking about needing to purchase a computer. He thought that I had a few intelligent recommendations, so he asked me to help him find one and maybe go for lunch. We went for a few lunches, but just as friends. He was very understanding and not pushy at all. He was a genuinely nice guy. I enjoyed the attention. At the same time, I also had a couple of other male friendships on the go. Tony, my fellow bartender at Zap's, was a good-looking guy. He was very shy, but became sort of a challenge to me. We slept together, but I could not get anything more from him emotionally. When he had me over to his house, he wanted to watch pornography. It was strictly a casual sex relationship. And each time, he played hard to get. I didn't respect myself for this relationship, but it was an empty distraction. One night, we played a game of truth or dare with my friend Jode and Tony's friend, Oscar. This was a first for me, as I had never played the game. Usually children or teenagers would play it at parties. And so, the dares began in short order, and ended with the switching of kissing partners. They even dared Jody and I to touch tongues. We tried, and as much as I loved Jode, that was not my cup of tea. No 'shades of gay', in this girl.

There was another guy, even more fleeting, named Luke. He had an earring, short brown hair, and slender build and I had met him at the bar Cactus Pete's. He drove a blue convertible and had bought a house with a few other guys in Lively while they were in school. He seemed very distracted, and the only thing I got from him, was a broken interior light in my Plymouth Sundance, and discomfort from when pubic hair was starting to grow back in after I let him shave it. I wish I had known then, the dangers of using someone else's razor, but ignorance is bliss, and I was lucky to not have acquired any Sexually Transmitted Diseases. I was enjoying being single, but I just wasn't satisfied by the physical relationships I was having. While mopping the floor behind the bar one day, a client at the bar commented to me, "You'll make someone a good wife, someday!" Wife equals housekeeper? Was that all that I was good for?

I soon applied to Don Cherry's Restaurant and Sports Bar because the tips were supposedly better, there. It was a nicer environment, with fairly nice managers, although one manager seemed to have a hate-on for me at first. It felt like I couldn't do anything right in his eyes. I worked my butt off to impress him, and finally, started to earn some praise. Word had it that he was canned for smoking marijuana on duty. No wonder he didn't notice how hard that I worked! Dan stopped by to my bar one night, with his ex-brother-in-law. Seeing him was shocking and brought up a whole bunch of feelings, that I didn't know I still had. He was kind, and very calm, and I'm not sure if he knew I'd be there. I felt frazzled. I never saw him again.

One day, Mark and John came in for lunch. I was able to sit with them for a bit, it was nice to see them again. Mark and I made a date to go out again. When Mark's name and number was on the answering machine again, Dad said, "Who is this Mark Thomas guy, that keeps calling?". I told him "Just a friend, Dad!". He replied, "He just wants to get into your pants!".

Against my Dad's approval, I moved into my own apartment, in walking distance from his blue house on Janet street. He didn't speak to me or visit for a bit as he was angry with me for leaving. Eventually he warmed up, and helped me find some cheap, pink furniture for it. It was terribly uncomfortable, but it was mine. Beth and her Dad painted my apartment for me. It was a rich, happy, sky blue, and the entire South side of my bedroom and the living room were all windows. It was really nice. I even bought myself a little white, deaf cat, and named her "Mishka". Her little claws kept sticking to the carpet, so I had to put newspaper down so that she could walk. She left hairy white clouds everywhere she went. She especially like to crawl under my bed covers to my feet for warmth.

One day, I went to the bar, Cactus Pete's with Mark and John, and had way too many drinks of vodka and orange juice (screwdrivers)... we went to the Burger joint drive through for Poutine, before dropping me to my apartment. I got sick that night. That was the point of going to the bars on weekends. You went to rid yourself of stress and just have fun! Then puke and swear you would never drink again! From then on, I couldn't eat there again, and nicknamed the restaurant "Burger Puke".

Mark offered me some pots and pans for my new place. He invited me to his house for dinner, after my shift at Don Cherries. I showed up in my black Don Cherries' uniform. He made me fried pickerel, homemade French fries and canned peas. It melted in my mouth, it was scrumptious! When he found out that I liked fishing too, he invited me to go fishing with him on Onaping Lake. I hadn't gone fishing since we went camping at Vermillion River Campground as a family, when BJ was still around. I missed it. Dad had an aluminum boat with a 9.9 horsepower Johnson motor, and we always remembered it fondly.

It was a hot day, when Mark took me fishing, and I had made this one piece cover up for my bathing suit. It was a floral one-piece short set with a zipper along the front torso and a V-neck. It was a very hot day, but I would need sunscreen if I were to remove it. I left it on, because I didn't want Mark to get the wrong idea. He baited my hook for me, which brought me right back to my childhood. I roasted, but had a really nice time, and as far as we were up the lake, I felt safe. I met Mark's Aunt Jackie and Uncle Roger, who had a camp on Onaping. Mark's aunt asked me how long we had been dating, and I blurted out, "No, we're just friends!".

Dad was very social. He had no problem meeting the ladies. Mom was a homebody, and hadn't really dated. One day, Mel and I entered Mom's profile in the local paper, the Northern Life's classified section, to encourage her to start dating. She seemed to enjoy getting inquiries, so I thought I'd give it a go, too! I read through the classifieds while there was nothing to watch on my two-channel black and white, twelve-inch TV, and found one that caught my eye, "Down to Earth Male, seeking..." "Hmmm!" I gave him a call. I made a date to meet this Mister Down to Earth at the annual Northern Lights Festival Boreal at Bell Park. When I arrived, I really wanted to turn right around, but said to myself "Don't be shallow!".

Mister Down-to-earth, had the look of a character from the cover of a Goosebumps novel. His front teeth aimed straight out of his head, and when he removed his sunglasses, his bulgy eyes, were looking everywhere but in the same direction. I stifled a gasp, and thought I just had to make some small talk for a while then take my leave. After fifteen minutes of shear agony, I said "Sorry! I have to go. Good-bye!" I beelined it to my apartment and had a huge sigh of relief when I closed and locked the door. What was I thinking? I am shallow.

Not a half hour later, the phone rang. It was Mark, who said "What are you doing?". "Nothing much" was my response. He continued to say that he was visiting friends on the lake and they would be going out in the Pontoon boat shortly, and would I like to join them for a ride? "Sure!" I replied, and made my way down to the agreed upon dock at Ramsey Lake and waited for my ride. As they eased up to the dock, Mark offered me his hand to help me aboard, and I met Sandy and Gord. A very nice couple. Gord was very quiet, as he piloted the boat as Sandy filled us in all kinds of gossip about who lives on Ramsey Lake. As we listened, we enjoyed wine, crackers and camembert cheese. I sat back, looked at Mark and had one of those moments where I realized ... Isn't he down to earth? Isn't this incredibly nice? Why haven't you thought of him this way, before?

This is a direct quote from my journal:

> *"He's the type of person that I could have a lot of fun with and trust completely. I've always said I wanted to be really good friends with the man I marry. Last night he said he want to eventually marry his best friend. We had a strange moment as we looked at each other after those words, almost like we knew what each other was thinking because it was, the same thought. I've been trying so hard to convince myself and my friends that Mark and I are just friends, and we are...but I think he might just be the one. I've been very determined not to follow in my parents' footsteps, as they lead to disaster. It seems many people get married based on a mutual lust and superficial friendship, but then find they have nothing in common and split up. That would not happen with us. One thing that I'm sure of with Mark (and I'm in no hurry), is*

that he cares for me a lot, would be a great companion and the fact that we are friends guarantees a mutual respect and trust for one another...hmmm...what a strange feeling this is."

It was the moment that everything changed, for me. Now, how would I let him know?

How do you change a relationship from "Just Friends", to more?

CHAPTER THREE

A Happy Wife

It was July 14, 1995. Mark and I were sitting on his green leather loveseat at his house in Garson, after an evening out with my friend Beth, and I kept stewing on how to start flirting with him. Finally, at his place later, I put my head on his knee. He bent over and kissed me. He was so gentle, and so sweet. It was scary, but also exciting. It was just a kiss, but a symbol of the beginning of a new journey.

The next week, Melanie and I took our very first flight anywhere. Dad sponsored our trip to St. John's, with Royal Air. It was a great deal at $250 for each of our return flights. Alejandro and his partner, André had an apartment in Toronto, so Mel and I drove the four-hour drive to Toronto, and stayed with Alejandro. Alejandro drove us to the airport, then next day for our flight. Our direct flight lasted only two and a half hours to St. John's, Newfoundland. Dad had taken Mel down east for four consecutive summers. I could never go, because he never planned ahead and I could never get the time off on such short notice. I have to admit, this made me a little jealous.

I hadn't been back since I was twelve years old. It was time. I was twenty-three, and Mel was a very hormonal seventeen. No sooner did the pilot announce that we would begin our descent, and the plane hit an air pocket. We all gasped as we dropped straight down. Who knows how many meters we plummeted, and I was surprised that the descent would be so direct! It may have lasted five seconds, but it was a scary moment for the two of us, clutching at our seats for safety. We exhaled and had a good, nervous laugh. We landed safely and Uncle Jim was there to pick us up.

Uncle Jim looked a bit like Dad, with a couple extra pounds, and a full head of shiny, sculpted, black hair. Dad was a good-looking man but pretty bald on top, with random single spikes of hair that stuck straight up, like peach fuzz, but not so dense. I told him "skin is in!" to try to get him to shave the comb-over hairdo. Jim was always a very warm and loving uncle always made us feel welcome. It was great to see him after all these years! It was less than an hour's drive to New Harbour, as we were going to stay at Uncle Jim and Jenna's place. We stayed a week, and for most of it, Mel took every opportunity to insult me. I tried my hardest to keep patient and calm, but I knew that my Aunts and Uncles didn't appreciate her arrogance towards me.

We also stayed at our Grandparents' house in Old Shop for a couple of those days. Nan had an accent that was a mixture of Scottish and Newfie. She spoke quietly and very quickly, so it was a little difficult to understand her, at first. But, she had nothing but love for us! No one really knew how old Nan was, as she kept herself so young. She was a hard worker. My Grandfather, we called him "Poppy", had passed away from a heart attack, years before. Nan continued to live in the same little house in which they raised their seven kids, but she was surrounded by her children. They had three children while in Inverness, Scotland. Dad, "Donald John", was their third child. Once Dad turned two, they moved to Newfoundland to very, very hard times. After moving to Newfoundland (The Rock),

Nan and Poppy had four more children. Most of Dad's siblings resided nearby, so it was always so lovely to visit and see them all.

We did get to spend some time with a few of our cousins. Aunt Dorothy, Dad's youngest sister, made us a traditional Newfie dinner of fish and brews, and took us out to a party at a local Hall. We danced and had a good time, and I think Mel may have had some booze. We stayed at Aunt Dorothy and Uncle John's place that night with cousins Briana and Denis. It worked out that we were there for the George Street Festival. My cousin Timothy, was in town visiting at the same time.

One night, Timothy picked me up at Nan's in his parents' shiny black car, and brought me out for dinner. I had a seafood platter, full of fresh fish, and shrimp. It was delicious. We left the restaurant and I made Timothy stop at the next gas station. I felt as all colour drained from my face, that my seafood was swimming quickly south. I made it just in time, and was relieved that it was a one-time deposit. I was then free to enjoy the rest of the evening.

We arrived in St. John's and found a place to park, and we walked downtown to George Street. The street was blocked from traffic, and lined with pubs and tons of people. Drinking on the street was okay, and you could go from one bar to the next. We had fun, and got caught up on many things. I was starting to feel a little tipsy, and made our way through the park towards the car. We hadn't seen each other since we were twelve, and he laughed when I reminded him how he and Scott terrified me at the Salmon hole. He said something flattering, and under the influence of the evening, all reason left me, and made yet another brilliant move. I kissed my cousin. We were sitting on some park bench. His chin was firm and bristly, and he didn't have very much flesh on his lips, I flashed to thinking that this must be what it felt like to kiss me, minus the stubble, and I pulled away. This was definitely not premeditated. At least it was just a kiss, but it would have been less complicated with a stranger.

The next night, the family had a gathering at our Aunt and Uncle's place, and Timothy had had a few drinks. I didn't want him making it obvious that something had happened, but he was really struggling with it. I was so embarrassed and mad at myself for my lack of self-control. I apologized and told him that I had someone back home that I wanted to start seeing. Maybe this was my subconscious testing to see if I truly wanted to give Mark and I a shot, and I used him. I just wanted to erase this, and pretend that it had never happened. After Mel and I returned home, I was resolved that Mark was definitely, the one for me. We dated for three months, and then I moved in. I had a few awkward conversations with Timothy, but felt like I had finally gotten the message across.

Mark had a house in Garson, that looked like a back-split. He and his parents, Fred and Harriet, had built a house together, as they planned to travel to Florida for the winters. It had the back-yard sloped up towards the highway, Falconbridge Road, and a flat garden levelled for Harriet. They were warm, wonderful people that made everyone feel welcome. Mark's parents lived in the large downstairs apartment, with two bedrooms. Mark was upstairs, in a three-bedroom level. The carpets were all turquoise and the walls, the first shade of pink. When Mark first bought it, it was for him and Wendy, his girlfriend of five years. No sooner did they move in, and they split up. The kitchen had white cupboards, and I liked that the kitchen had two entrances as it reminded me of my Nan's apartment. It just felt right. He made my life complete, and I liked who I was with him. Our cats got along pretty well, he had this brownish-orangey Persian named after his Dad, "Fred", who was always crying for ham "hhhaaaaamm".

I found Fred, the cat hard to get to know, this cat was a cranky old bugger. But, he had a soft spot for my little Mishka that would cuddle with him. My Mishka loved to stay warm, and one hot summer night, I was sleeping in a tank top, and I guess it had twisted while I slept. I had the most unusual and uncomfortable dream, and woke to found my Mishka, latched onto my nipple and palpating my breast with her front paws. I loved that cat, but I still threw her off of the bed. From then on, I made sure to don pajamas with better nipple coverage.

Mark was nine years older than me, but he was young at heart. I was an old soul.

I always believed that things happened for a reason. Had I been more successful and stayed at Queen's, I may never have moved back home, would not have been working at Zap's and never would have met him. As far as past relationships and mistakes, these were really important events, too. I would never have been interested or gone for Mark, until I was ready to see how perfect he really was for me.

Fred, Mark's Dad, was tall and had white hair receding from the crown. He wore glasses and had a soft voice. He referred to Harriet as "Bud", or "Chicken", but "Bud" or "Buddy", was how everyone in the extended family knew her. Harriet and her two sisters had nicknames, Florence was "Tiny", and Wilma was "Billie". I couldn't bring myself to call Harriet "Buddy", being that she was kind of a Mother-in-law to me and it didn't sound respectful. She said she didn't mind me calling her "Harriet", so I did, but the family didn't know to whom I was referring when I would call her by her given name. Harriet called Freddy "Bay". She was a fantastic cook. She would make enough to feed an army, there was always leftovers. She would make a lazy cabbage roll that she called "Yebrig", and the best homemade soups. Her Coconut Cream Pies were to die for. She would make a regular one with white sugar, then she would make one with Splenda, as a sugar substitute, for her Diabetic husband. He'd always sneak the real one after, on top of the sugar free pie. He loved to cheat with desserts. Harriet had a sparkle in her eye, and knew what he was up to. She loved to laugh, and she had a young heart! They loved going out to the Bingo. If you said, "Want to go the Casino? She'd be ready to go in no time. Harriet used to buy bags of chips and hide them, because she knew that Mark would come and try to find them when he had the munchies. They both seemed to enjoy that game.

Mark had two older sisters, Betty and Mary. Betty, eight years older than Mark and single, had become a Family Physician. She was a wonderful and very generous person. She was also a fantastic, fancy cook, and would buy all the groceries she would need, and come and cook for us. I never liked mushrooms, until she made us stuffed portabella mushrooms, with peppers, onions, hamburger, spices and melted cheese. She made wonderful risotto and breaded yams, that you dip into sour cream. My favourite treat, was when she would flambé bananas for Bananas Foster dessert. She was warm too, but hard to read, as she wasn't one to make much conversation.

Mary, was nine years older than Mark, and was married to Romeo and had two girls, Valerie and Sarah. Valerie was the same age as my sister Mel, and Sarah was nine years younger. They all lived in Sault Ste Marie, Ontario, and Romeo worked for Algoma Steel. Mary was more of a traditional cook, like her Mom, and equally fantastic. I absolutely loved her strawberry-rhubarb pies! I was so impressed at her use of tapioca as a thickener for her pies.

Family get togethers were delicious! One year I offered to put Harriet's two coconut cream pies in our fridge, as hers was full, but I was wearing the big green dinosaur slippers she had just given me for Christmas. I slipped on the third step going up, with a pie in each hand. The pies landed safely, right side up on the second step from the top, and my ribs took the brunt of the fall. I had bruised ribs for over two months afterwards, as I had landed on the metal nosing of the stairs, but those were the best coconut cream pies, ever!

When the next door neighbours split up, they gave their Black and White Alaskan Malamute Dog to Mark's Dad. The dog's name was Timber, and he was both beautiful and intimidating to look at. He had thick white and black fur, and each eye was a different colour, one blue, and one brown. Mark's Dad was always the one who walked him every day, and always bought a bag of food to have on hand for his visits after his walk. This walk did wonders for his blood sugar. The dog had to spend most of his time outside, so Fred built him a doghouse. He was just too hot to stay indoors. It was comforting when we camped with him, as he would prowl all night. We knew that if he wasn't excited, we were safe. His parents used to have a camp on French River, but sold it and still enjoyed spending time at Uncle Roger and Aunt Jackie's camp, on Onaping. They loved spending time together at the camp, playing dice or double solitaire, and going fishing for pickerel, also known as "walleye". They were very close.

Mark spent many years getting to know that long, rocky lake and stored his boat at Ladouceur's Landing, just past the town of Cartier. We went camping up the lake all together with our tents. We had enough tarps to keep everything dry, and good sealable coffee tubs to keep the toilet paper dry. The toilet was always down a path, and was usually a plywood box, that previous campers had left, some of them had a toilet seat, some just a hole. We could tent in just about any conditions, but tried not to go in the beginning of July when the black flies and mosquitos were at their prime. We had our full rain suits so we could stay out and fish in the rain, Mark always put my bait on for me, and took the fish off of my hook. The best was when we hit a 'honey hole', which meant we'd catch fish with every cast. We could only keep so many, so I got tired of catching to just release them again. My rain suit was purple, and it had a million pockets. It could get pretty hot wearing it though. If there was a warm rain, it didn't breathe at all. We enjoyed the campfire at night before retiring into our tents. Mark used to snore pretty loudly, which used to scare me when I thought I'd hear something outside. I worried that if it was a bear, Mark's snore was like a beacon to invite the attack. But, it never happened, and I learned to relax a bit and trust the dog.

Mark's Aunt Jackie and Uncle Roger were just as warm as Mark's parents, and great to be around. Roger was Harriet's brother. His eyes sparkled too. We loved spending time with them. Roger was very talented and built their log camp. He had recovered from an alcohol addiction, which plagued several uncles on that side of the family. They had some pretty crazy stories from way back when. During Roger's recovery, he whittled amazing wooden chains, to keep his hands busy. They made for interesting decor hanging from the beams at camp. As their three kids grew and had their own kids, he built another camp for just for the two of them, so they could have their quiet space. Often, they'd let us spend our holidays at the main camp. This was the best place to unwind and found a special place in our hearts.

In the fall, my cousin Scott left the Rock (Newfoundland) in search of welding work, he stayed with us in our spare room for about a month. Mark changed employers as a sales rep for another Food chain. He'd been going for days on end for his training, and neither of us liked being apart for that long. We brought Scott to camp, and he really enjoyed being on the water. I think it made him homesick. He was a homebody too, like me. Scott wasn't finding anything permanent, and Mark started to get a little distant. Dad even asked me about what the problem was, were we having relationship problems or was it having Scott there for so long... It might have been, but I never really found out. Scott left soon thereafter, and left us a nice letter when he left:

"Thanks Mark & Jan (Sis)!!

You guys have been great. Why does this hurt so much? Mark, you've been like family to me and I appreciate that. Say "Bye", to your Mom and Dad for me, and a "Thanks!" also! And Sis, thank-you so much for all your love and support just when I always needed it. You will always be the Sister I never had and I will miss you so much! Say "Bye" to Uncle Donald for me. He has been a big help to me and I love him. And say "Bye" to your Mom and Mel which I should have seen more than I did.

Luvs you guys!

Your Brother, Scott.

P.s. Mark, take care of my Sis and if you plan to marry her, let me be the first to know."

I was doing very well at College, maintaining a 4.0 average, and happier than ever with Mark. One night he asked me if I would marry him someday. I said I would, someday. That's the first time we ever discussed it.

School was mostly business for me and not a social outlet. There was only one girl that I hung around with. I referred to her as, "Crazy Corrie". We had some conflicts. I really liked to avoid conflicts altogether, but I had to learn to be assertive and stand up for myself. She was a "mature" student, three or four years older than me, with two young kids at home that she was trying to support by going back to school. I respected her for that. She had an abusive partner that she left, and that must have been so difficult. She was boisterous and smiley. She was fun one minute and if you looked at her sideways, she'd chew you up one side and down the other regardless of who was watching.

Somehow or other, she was my closest friend at school, as most everyone else was still wet behind the ears from high school. There were only twelve of us, in this class. What I didn't respect, as it was against my new rules, was her relationship with this married Lebanese man, named "Cam". Cam was not an attractive man in my books and didn't seem to think highly of women. He used her for sex, wasn't very kind, and left her money in the morning. I thought she was prostituting herself for the kids. She was only sleeping with him at the time, and was really upset that I didn't like him. I guess I would have rather her think that I disliked him, or seemed to, than to let on that it was really her that I was beginning to dislike. I wanted to distance myself from her. She put me down regularly, and quite publicly. It was very humiliating. One day she advised me quite loudly that my mouth looked like an anus. The lipstick trend at the time, was a brown liner around glossy lips. The gloss had worn off. She considered me to be a good friend, and confided in me often, but the light in her eyes went out whenever the conversation turned to me. This was a one-sided friendship. Eventually, I followed Kristi's example from grade six, and I stopped talking to her. I actually acted mad, and gave her the cold shoulder. I didn't know what else to do, but she was draining me. I no longer wanted to be her confidante.

Mark's distant moods resurfaced now and again, it was almost cyclic. I would bend over backwards to make Mark stop being distant. Usually sex seemed to bring him back, I could manage this, if it would keep him happy. I did love sex with Mark, he was no musician, but he knew how to play my instruments! We practiced much and he gave amazing orgasms. I learned how to trigger my own orgasms, which had never really occurred during sex before. As much as I loved the sex, I grew away from needing it. I lived for the moments of random, loving contact. Like when he'd brush the hair from my eyes, or hold my hand, or say things like "My wife is my life." I was more needful of the intimacy before and after sex. It's what I needed more than anything, to feel secure. However, when I had been drinking, I was more likely to seek out the horizontal 'Polka'.

Mark thought differently than my parents and I, and many times I had to explain his moods to them. They were sensitive too, to his behavioural changes. They would take it personally, or assume that we were having problems. Mark's family were not physical people, and sometimes they appeared grumpy, when they weren't. I found myself talking too much, to fill the void, and try to make them smile. Mark had no idea how much my mood depended on his.

On July 14, 1997, Mark and I came out from camp to go to dinner for our second anniversary together. We went to the restaurant downtown, next to Cactus Pete's called "Alexandria's". We had a nice meal, and over my chocolate eruption dessert, he asked me "What do we do, now?". I said, "What do you mean" (of course, I play dumb, because I want to hear what he will say). His response was "What do you want to do in the next ten years?". Without much thought, and no hesitation, I said "Have kids". That started it. He said, "That's the thing, do we get married or have kids and just live together?" He emphasized that he wanted to do the right thing, so he said "Let's get married, I'm ready." "Okay", I said with all of my heart, no reluctance, no hesitation, and no doubt whatsoever. I knew this was right. He apologized for not having a ring for me when he proposed, but said he'd been looking and wanted me to pick it out. The only problem was that he didn't want us to tell anyone about our engagement until I got the ring. It was hard to keep it on the down low, especially when over dinner one night, Dad said, "If you marry my daughter, I'll give you my truck!". A Dowry!

When we first started discussing wedding plans, we thought of something small, even just eloping to Jamaica or Las Vegas and then come back for a reception. We both liked the month of September, and I would be finished my three-year program, by then.

We announced our engagement to the family at Christmas. It was a very memorable moment as he bent down on one knee to put the ring on my finger, a pear-shaped diamond engagement ring.

What was going to be the most wonderful year, soon took a turn. Mark's Dad was anemic the year before and they didn't find the cause until a specialist had a scope performed to his both ends. Colon cancer was detected at his caecum, by the pancreas. Everything proceeded pretty fast from there. His ultrasound pre-surgery showed some fuzz on his liver. During the removal of the affected portion of the colon, a needle biopsy confirmed extensive invasion of cancer cells in the liver. A few days later, the bone scan showed five metastases in five different bones. He had been having leg pain. He was given shot of morphine and sent home eight days post-surgery. He was quite disoriented. After a six-hour sound sleep, we decided to wake him for supper. He didn't wake and was in a diabetic coma. We called the ambulance. The emergency Doctor said that he had suffered a minor heart attack, and a partial lung collapse.

The cardiologist later confirmed that there had been damage to the liver and not the heart, due to some drug he had been given.

It also made it difficult to keep his glucose up. He'd never been hypoglycemic. He was given less than six months to live. The morphine seemed to be making him very confused, and Mark's sister Betty, convinced the Doctors to change his pain meds to a Durazek patch, instead. His liver enzymes normalized and so did his sugar. I took time off my placement at the hospital lab to help and to be with Mark during this difficult time. Mark was not comfortable at the hospital.

Harriet cared for Fred at home for as long as she could. She had nurses come in, and had a special bed assembled in the living room. He didn't last six months. He was failing quickly and too much for Harriet to manage. He went back to the hospital. We saw him on his last day. I went with Mark. Mark stood dumbfounded and full of grief by the wall at the door of the bed, and I sat next to Fred, held his hand and told him that Mark was there. It was in March, when Fred lost his battle.

Mark said something to me, that really saddened me. That I had no friends of my own. I used to have lots of friends and anyone I really grew close to, moved away. Jody was still in town, but she never wanted to put any effort into getting together. I gave up, as it was exhausting. I guess, I'd become a little too critical and less patient. Maybe, I was too picky, or too distrustful, or had unreasonable expectations. Or, maybe I'd just been too busy! I was working all day at placement, and three to four nights at Don Cherries. This made for some very long days 7:00 am to Midnight, some days, and some days even later. But I never partied after work, as I did at Zap's. I used to feel ill going in for the 7:00 shift, as we had to hurry up, and get on the floors to take morning blood collections. I used to get so nervous that I'd get diarrhea. I was working so much, that I got very skinny. Almost scary skinny, for me, at 5-foot-4-inches and 130 pounds.

I finished school with a 4.0 average but hadn't yet been hired on as a Medical Laboratory Technologist. Instead, I got a job at MDS Laboratories as a "Laboratory Support Clerk", getting paid a meagre $9.74 an hour. They kept telling me how impressed they were with me to have been trained in only two weeks as opposed to the expected three months. This was a private lab, that allowed most of the testing to be done by Technicians, and only hired a couple of Technologists to oversee and troubleshoot. They didn't make as much money here as they did in the hospital lab, so I was really hoping to get in when they had an opening.

Mark was having abdominal pains since his father's death, and booked a colonoscopy. He said "what if they find out something before we go away?". I went with Mark for his colonoscopy and was worried that the Doctor's secretary had not corrected her mistake having previously scheduled Mark for a vasectomy. I peeked over the list on the counter, and saw colonoscopy beside Mark's name. Thank God! No news is good news, and we didn't hear anything bad before heading to Vegas for the Wedding.

Saturday, September 26, 1998

The morning of September 26, 1998, there was quite a bit of fog. Dad's girlfriend, Renée, picked us up at 5:45 a.m. to bring us to the airport. Our Air Ontario flight to Toronto was delayed by one hour, and we didn't lift off until 7:30 a.m. It was like National Lampoon's vacation, as we raced through the airport in Toronto to find our baggage and get through customs. We got business class seats, which was such a treat, and settled in for the ride. I couldn't get over the view down there, all green patches in a perfect circle, or part of a perfect circle. The mountains look like they were pictures in an atlas...bumpy. We watched the Truman Show on the online entertainment. Lunch was very nice for airplane food. I had fruit, salad, nice cheese, camembert-like, a bun, pasta with scallops (and only 2 shrimps). Mark had a steak filet, that wasn't bad, he said. Mark's toe was tingling. I hoped his Gout wasn't acting up again. Upon our arrival in L.A, we were to call "Gabriel" to pick us up and bring us to our Volkswagen Westfalia camper. This is so exciting!

On Sunday, September 27

Driving from Barstow KOA campground, California, on Hwy 15N to Las Vegas...

The night before we drove to Victorville. We were going to stay at the KOA campground, but it was right next to the highway and not all that impressive. We were in the desert, and there weren't many trees above 2-3 feet. We chose to head to the next KOA site on the way to Barstow. There were some growing pains with the camper. Our first designated campsite, #55, didn't have any hydro, and it was dark. So, I went in my little spring dress and sandals to talk to the girl at the registration desk, who had a marked-up chin, a brush cut and tattoos all the way down her arm. She looked at me like I had three heads when I told her we didn't have any hydro-so I said, e-l-e-c-t-r-i-c-i-t-y! Ohhh! These words were synonymous in Canada, but not in the U.S.A. It was also rather intimidating when we first pulled up and the place was bustling with military everywhere. I was wishing I had changed out of my short dress...you just never know! We next had a hard time figuring out the fridge. The propane didn't seem to be working and we needed to keep our yogurt cool. We figured out how to work it with the electricity as a power source. Hurray! We figured out how to use the propane in the morning, but the fridge would shut off every time we hit a bump in the road. The next night we stayed at the Luxor hotel in Las Vegas, and would stay there until Thursday night.

Monday, September 28, 1998

The Luxor hotel was in the shape of a black glass pyramid at one end of Las Vegas Blvd. It was beautiful. Our room number was 17103. We were joined by Mom and Mel, Betty and Harriet, friends Duncan and Ginette and Betty's friends Cathy and Jean-Pierre. Everyone had a room at the Luxor, except Dad and Renée stayed next door at the New York, New York hotel. Mom was pretty sick from the jet lag and stayed in her room, the first night. The rest of us went for dinner at the Tropicana. When someone complained about her steak, at an adjacent table, Betty and Duncan saw the waiter slip into a nearby booth, flip the steak over with his hands, and bring the plate back to her and said "How's that? We chose not to complain about our food. We all piled into the Volkswagen camper to get down the strip to see Cirque du Soleil. It was an incredible spectacle.

Tuesday, September 29, 1998

Mark and I had to go into town, to get a marriage license. Once the business was out of the way, it was time to enjoy.

I'd been playing blackjack with Mark. The money didn't get used up so quickly that way. Renée made about $200 on the slots from her first 50 cents. Dad went crazy in Vegas, he sure likes his gambling! But he's actually done okay. I donated $60 to those hungry machines because I got greedy. I thought I'd better stick to the tables. Mark and I decided to rest up. I needed my beauty sleep for the big day!

Wednesday, September 30, 1998

I just got back from my Swedish massage... Ahhh! How wonderful, I felt so beautiful and womanly. Ester, my masseur was telling me what I was like based on what my "body told her". Generally, that I was not as shy as I used to be, that I have a sore back and sore ears, and that I read a lot, etc... wow!

Mom and Mel had a massage too, and we were all skinny dipping in the hot tub, before our massages. That was awkward. Especially, when we didn't have any towels.

Once we got our hair done, and my headpiece secured in place. I felt like a Princess. We got dressed and picked up by limousine at the entrance to the hotel. Since it was just a ten-person limo, Dad and Renée drove our 'Love Bug' behind us. We arrived at Red Rock Canyon in about fifteen minutes, and we had a Minister of Religious Science, a Reverend Richard Walter, who gave us the choice of modern versus traditional vows. I voted for traditional, and he also asked how I wanted him to say my name. I asked him to call me Jan-Andrea, in some strange way it made me feel like Nan was there, too. Dad walked me up the hill and we dodged donkey dung, and got my headpiece snagged in a tree, but we made it, and the scenery was beautiful with the sandy mountains in pink hues. Duncan was our best man, and Mel was my Maid of Honour. It was a beautiful ceremony. The one thing that distracted me from crying for a while was the mosquito that landed and started feeding on the Ministers' upper lip.

The Minister recited the following passage from Corinthians 13:

"Love is patient, love is kind, and is not jealous;
love does not brag and is not arrogant,
does not act unbecomingly; it does not seek its own, is not
provoked, does not take into account a wrong suffered,
does not rejoices in unrighteousness, but rejoices with the truth;
bears all things, lives things, hopes all things, endures all things
Love never fails; but if there are gifts of prophecy, they
will be done away; if there are tongues, they will cease,
if there is knowledge it will be done away.
For we know, in part, and we prophesy in part;
but when the perfect comes, the partial will be done away
When I was a child, I used to speak as a child, think as a child, reason
as a child; When I became a man, I did away with childish things.
For now we see in a mirror dimly, but then face to face; Now I know in
part, but then I shall know fully just as I also have been fully known.
But now abide in faith, hope, love, these three;
but the greatest of these is love."

Mark adjusted an unruly strand of hair next to my face and when he said his vows, his voice cracked. Then I had a lot of trouble saying my vows. Not that I didn't want to get through them, but was so moved by the happiness of the moment. Besides Fred and Mary's family not being there, everyone else that we loved the most was there to share it and it was perfect! It didn't help that Mom and Dad were also tearing up. Once we signed on the dotted line, we cracked open the champagne and went back to dine at the buffet at the Luxor. For our wedding night, we were spent, we gambled a bit, and then just went to sleep. I had a beautiful negligée, and was disappointed that I didn't get the chance to wear it on my wedding night. I had a few too many drinks though, so it probably would have been counter-productive.

Thursday, Oct. 1, 1998

Almost everyone from our party, left on Thursday, and we spent one last night with Dad and Renée, checking out New York, New York and the many hotels on the strip. We were anxious to get on with our honeymoon the next day.

We set off, just the two of us on the Friday, heading north in Nevada in our Love Bug. I had put my blue garter on the rearview mirror. Mark grew a little sleepy, and since he was the only one that could drive a standard, we pulled over at the "Cottontail Ranch", which looked like a roadhouse restaurant. There was dirt bike racing nearby. I had to pee, so I made my way to the entrance, and walked in the first set of doors. I walked into a very small foyer with another door which had a small porthole window. On the door was a sign that read "Ring bell for pleasure". The light in my head went on, and I realized, this was not the best place to tinkle. It was a brothel! We were just on the corner of Hwy 95 and Hwy 266. The scenery was mostly desert and continuous mountain ranges. It was no wonder Mark was tired. This place was giving me the creeps, so I held my bladder and bided my time in the 'Love Bug', while Mark slept. I kept the doors locked.

We made our way to the High Sierras and stayed at the "Creekside Campground". The scenery was beautiful, and we enjoyed being able to stop anytime, anywhere and make a meal in our camper. We made soup and grilled cheese and Spanish onion sandwiches (a camp favourite). We found a thank-you note in an empty cooler bottle from Dad and Renée. I guess they enjoyed our 'Love Bug' after all!

We froze when we stayed at Tuolumne Meadows. At first, we thought it was funny that everyone was dressed in mittens, toques and winter jackets. Turns out we were the dumb ones! We were at 9000 ft above sea level in the mountains. We woke up with ice on the windshields. We were told that there was a very active bear population and to make sure there wasn't any food or cosmetics left in our camper. There were 'bear boxes' installed at each campsite, meant to store all food and make-up. We didn't sleep very well due to the cold and listening for bears. When Mark started the engine to warm us up, I was worried that since it was a standard, and we were parked on a hill just above of a two-man pup tent, that we were going to roll right over them.

The next night we spent down in the Lower Pines campsite of Yosemite Valley. There were several VW campers there, and we really fit in. We met a nice man that gave us some instructions on how to fill the propane and empty the used water from the sink. The redwood trees were huge, and it was much warmer here. I put my foot in my mouth around the campfire that night and embarrassed Mark with my response when a young German couple had told us their story about having just arrived to the US and having all of their belonging stolen. I slurred, "Welcome to America"! This was particularly embarrassing to Mark, since the other two couples, a yuppie couple and an older couple that we were sitting with, were American. *'Please ignore the drunk Canadian.'*

The scenery was so lush and beautiful coming out of the mountains from Yosemite. I was not too impressed with the winding, steep roads, since I was hungover from the little party we had around the campfire the night before.

We drove through wine country and were very pleased with the warmth we encountered. We stopped in Oakdale to do some laundry at "Launderland". From there we drove to Napa Valley and stopped at three different wineries.

We stayed next at the Bothe National Park, between St. Helena and Calistoga. At this park there were no bear boxes to hide food, but there were warning about poison oak "Leaves of three, let them be", ticks and yellow jackets. I didn't know what yellow jackets were, but assumed them to be like wasps or hornets. We didn't wander. We drank some wine that we bought for Peju winery and finally had our own campfire and played crazy eights with the used blackjack cards from Vegas, before calling it a night. Unfortunately, there were no friendly campers nearby. We drove through Calistoga, but I wished we had stayed there...There was an inviting sign that read: "Land of hot springs and mud baths".

From Calistoga we drove through Sonoma, then to Petaluma. Duncan told us that his parents stayed here, and recommended it. It was very close to San Francisco, and stayed there for two nights. We signed up for a comprehensive tour/experience of San Francisco, from 8:00 to 4:30 the next day.

We had a wonderfully chatty tour guide, named Nancy. She was full of fascinating information. There were twelve tourists in the big van, and Nancy had a speaker phone so we could hear her loud and clear. Our first stop was on the Golden Gate bridge, but it was a little foggy. Then we went to the Japanese tea gardens where I sampled Jasmine tea. It was very nice, even Mark liked it. We also got to ride the cable cars. Nancy put us all on at one spot, she said be assertive and smile! She told us to get off once we saw her smiling face, which we managed to do without any problem. We spent some time on touristy Pier 39, and ate at Isabella's Restaurant and had tiger prawns and sourdough bread. Nancy showed us three styles of houses, we got to experience the bumpy hill seen in many movie car chases, and the house used in the filming of the movie "Mrs. Doubtfire". We went to Chinatown, and went into a fortune cookie manufacturer on Ross Ave. They were hot off the press. She asked if we wanted "Sexy ones". We said "Sure!". I figured it was her accent only that made the word sound like "sexy", but no, that's what she meant. The fortunes inside were supposed to perverted, but I found them peculiar. i.e. "Fu Ling Yu Says: 90% of men who try Camels still prefer women."

Before leaving, we got to walk beneath the Golden Gate bridge and we boarded the van to head back to Petaluma eating chocolate and listening to "I left my heart in San Francisco". It was a wonderful tour!

We tried finding a sports bar in Petaluma. We were craving chicken wings, but they only had "Fried Chicken". We were tired and cooked up some Hamburger Helper in the camper instead.

After a good night's rest, we headed for Hwy 1 South. We drove to Monterey. We walked around Fisherman's wharf and the Cannery Row and drove through Pacific Grove looking for a deal on a suite, but decided to see what Carmel was like. Clint Eastwood used to be the Mayor of Carmel. We found an Inn, called "Hofsa's House", and paid a little more than it was worth. It was very old, and creaky, but it was quaint. We checked out Clint Eastwood's bar, the Hog's Breath Inn, and walked around Carmel for a bit. We then drove to Monterey for something to eat.

We packed up the next morning and headed back North. Unfortunately, the boardwalk in Santa Cruz was closed. We had to drop off the RV that evening at 6:00 pm in San Francisco. Our flight was for midnight from San Francisco Airport.

Since we were flying business class, we enjoyed the comforts of the "Continental Room" to rest and enjoy free beverages and food until our late flight. I needed complete darkness, quiet, and a comfy pillow to sleep, so there was no way I would sleep on the red eye flight home. Nevertheless, we had a great trip.

It was wonderful to get away, but so very nice to be home. We were planning a reception a couple of weeks later, on November 14th. On Halloween, Timber crawled out from under the fence that Mark had built to let him run in the backyard. When Mark and I found out that Timber had dug his way out, I went looking for him by foot, and Mark took my car. We searched, and searched. Mark picked me up on the highway and we went for another look together. When we came back, we saw him on the road. We had just missed him. He was lying, in the turning lane to our subdivision with his eyes open, mouth open and a little blood around his left eye. He was still warm, but definitely gone. Mark especially had a hard time. He was depressed all day and told me he felt 'dead' inside. I think he also felt he'd disappointed his Dad. We buried Timber in the backyard. I would never forget the sight of Mark picking Timber's body up out of my trunk, his whole posture rounded towards the dog and he sobbed as he carried him up to the top of the yard where the three of us, Harriet, Mark and I had dug his grave. It was so hard because we loved him, it was even harder to watch Mark. Maybe he was now with his rightful owner. We planted two pines atop him. It was awful.

I arranged a visit with a local dog breeder to see new Golden Retriever puppies. I was going to keep it a secret, but the breeder had left a message on our machine and Mark intercepted it. Once I told him about it, he told me he was looking at retrievers while he was in Timmins. We went together to see the last puppy of the nine-week-old litter and bought her on the spot. It felt more like an adoption though, with all of the papers to sign and pictures of her show Dad and Show Mom. We felt like parents. We named her "Bailey". While we were getting ready for the reception, we had newspapers all over the house, in case of puppy accidents. Becky came and stayed with us for the reception. It was so great to see her after so many years! As soon as everyone walked in Mark and I were at the entrance to welcome them and to let them know how things were to go for the evening. We told them to help themselves to the wine and food. We decorated the Garson Community Centre with balloons, gold and burgundy, filled with helium and connected to opposing tables with 40 Tess fishing lines making an archway which became the dance floor. We served free booze and were pleasantly surprised at how little people drank. We also bottled wine, a Cabernet Sauvignon and a Chardonnay with our personalized labels. "Announcing our Marriage Jan-Andrea and John Mark Thomas were wed at Red Rock Canyon in Las Vegas September 30, 1998". We had such a great time! Then Mark and Rob got up giving Ron and Rich a break and they played a tune. Mark sang, "Downtown Came Uptown" by David Wilcox. He was tone deaf, but it was cute.

Then Mark started his speech. He described the beginning of us as a fairy tale with a twist. It was quite romantic and was really neat to hear how he described it in front of everyone, almost rehearsed but very natural and fun. I followed his lead and by this time, I was three shades to the wind, so I don't quite remember what I said. I wasn't sure even before what I was going to say and figured I'd wait and see what my hubby would say. I did make mention of Dad's comment that when I told him Mark was just a friend, and he had said that he just wanted to get into my pants. I told him now, "I guess you were right!". The crowd enjoyed the comment. I also mentioned that it had been a tough year and we wished Fred could have been there with us. The rest was a blur, and not quite so eloquent as Mark's speech. Melanie then got up and brought tears to my eyes, followed by Mark's best man Duncan, who ended on a fun note. The band then continued and we asked the disk jockey (DJ) to start with our song "Love will Keep us alive" by the Eagles. For the bands' last song, they asked Mark and I to get up and dance. We looked at each other thinking, "no... the DJ is supposed to play our song first!" We went to the dance floor and the band played our song! "Love will keep us alive". They didn't now that was the song, and they swore they had not consulted with the DJ! Perhaps, it was fate! I took it as another symbol that we were meant to be. It was pretty neat how it worked out. The band was great, and the DJ had everyone dancing all night.

Mark's uncle Pat insisted that we open his gift right away. He had mouth painted a beautiful picture and personalized it with Calligraphy which Read "Congratulations Jan and Mark September 30, 1998." Pat was in a wheelchair due to MS. It was such a special gift!

We eased right into married life, though calling him my "husband", sounded so peculiar at first. Mark always impressed me on his ability to make and keep friends. He seemed like a friend superhero, with his ease at nurturing his relationships. This was so foreign to me, and it was a revelation. His friends became my friends, and we had great get-togethers, dinners, and neighbourhood gatherings. Mark was like the glue to our close neighbours and was happiest when we had company. The more the merrier. Mark would invite people over in the blink of an eye. He was very spontaneous.

I learned to ease off a bit on the house cleaning rules, because I was stressed that the house was never clean enough for company. Mark kept reminding me, that they were coming to visit us, not to inspect the house. I had my pride. I could clean like a mad woman in short order, the bathroom and the kitchen, at least, and a quick tidy of everything else. And every single time, at the very end of the night, I'd be glad we had our company. It was always a happy ending, and our life was full of friendship and love. People are what make life worth living. This is where most fairy tales would end, but we are Humans, after all, and life is constantly changing.

CHAPTER FOUR

Gambling for Children

Mark's friend Trevor and his wife had broken up because "she changed", once the kids came along. I really didn't want to change, but I really wanted kids. First, I needed a job.

As soon as the Laurentian hospital had an opening, I went in for an interview and was hired on the spot. I was finally getting a job in the field in which I had been trained. I was hired as a temporary part-time Core Lab, Medical Laboratory Technologist, to rotate in all of the departments in the Laboratory. This included morning collections and then Blood bank, Hematology, Chemistry, and Microbiology. This was the laboratory where I had my placement during school. It was a dream come true, minus the full time or permanent status. I got over my fear of morning blood collections and got pretty good at them, since we had some very difficult cancer patients. Some had veins like rubber bands from radiation treatments.

The money was great, starting at $18 per hour with additional pay in lieu of benefits and shift premiums. A far cry from my $3.10/

hour from my first job at 'Sweet and Saucey-Pizza and Donut Shop'! Crazy Corrie was also hired, but at the other hospital. Phew! We had three hospitals at the time, the Laurentian, the General and the Memorial. The shift work was tricky, but I was young, and flexible.

We were in the midst of putting a stone patio and interlocks around the back yard where the driveway passed by the left side of the house, and into the back yard. The front yard looked like a used car lot, with my cherry red Plymouth Sundance, the green Toyota Camry, Mark's new silver VW Jetta, Mark's Dad's royal blue Grand Marquis, and two boats. We also had piles of dirt and crusher dust for the interlock project. We were trying to sell my Plymouth Sundance, Mark's Dad's car, boat and motor in the local Bargain Hunter magazine. Harriet got her driver's license, and Mark helped her to buy a tan Toyota Corolla, to scoot around in. The Grand Marquis, I nicknamed as the "Hovercraft". It was just too big for her.

I loved being married to Mark, but due to my insecurity, I was having a hard time whenever he would have a bad day, or was unusually quiet. I always took it personally. Why did I have to be so insecure? I would keep on my people pleaser hat, and do my best to bring him around. Sex usually cured it.

Being in sales, Mark was usually out of town a couple of nights each week. It was nice to have the little alone time, which made me so excited for his return. Seeing him walk through the door always put a smile on my face. When my shifts allowed, I was able to join Mark on some of his sales meeting trips with other reps and store owners and their significant others. These were fun, because the company spoiled the spouses with activities while the associates were in meetings.

There was one in June 1999, at Cleveland's House in the Muskokas. It was our third visit to this resort with this company. Since my first visit, I'd been in love with this flowering bush that had the most delicious smell and white flowers... I suspected it to be a Mock Orange of some sort. I planted one in our backyard, and I hoped it would be the same as the one at the resort.

I gained ten pounds since I finished school and stopped working two jobs, and had to go shopping for a bathing suit in Port Carling while in the Muskokas. I also splurged and bought myself a two-piece turquoise floral sarong skirt and matching tank top. It felt so nice to get all dressed up. And it was perfect for our nice dinner that night at the resort. During dinner, the server was taking her time getting back to us and one of the people at our table wanted a coffee refill. I took it upon myself to grab the coffee thermos from the wait stand as it was just behind me. It was just a little too far to reach, so I got up to grab it. As I turned to place the pot on the table and sit back down, my skirt started to unwind. It unwrapped enough to show most of my leg, maybe even my underwear to the guy sitting next to Mark's empty chair (Mark was in the restroom). I was so embarrassed, I felt like such a Hillbilly. I followed my performance with tossing my salad across the table and slapping my plate with my knife as my fingers slipped from my grasp of the cutlery. When Mark returned to the table, the man sitting next to Mark, said to him with a gleam in his eye "You have a really nice wife".

We left pretty early the last morning, and headed for Bracebridge to visit my cousin, Scott. He had left his wife and two kids in Newfoundland for a three-month well-paying job here with the guarantee of his old job upon his return to the Rock. It must have been so hard for him to leave when his youngest, Desirée, was just a newborn. It was nice to see him, we were only thirty kilometers away, so I had to make the effort. Mark was disappointed that we had to drive a little more that day, but I appreciated his humoring me, as I didn't get to see my extended family as easily as he could.

Mark called me to join him for a night away the end of June, 1999, and we had rented the "Honeymoon suite" Cabin #4 at the Wee point resort on Manitoulin Island. They were very rustic cottages, not too far from Manitowaning where Mark was changing over a furniture store. Mark was extraordinary at giving directions, and I had no problem finding the furniture store to meet him for lunch upon my arrival. After lunch, he brought me on what felt like a wild goose chase, my car following his down these very rough back roads. The first one, I thought was to bring us to our camp, but it was to visit Randy's camp. The store owner. I was sure my car would bottom out. After a very long drive we picked up Randy's brother's Sea Doo and headed back the tedious way we came. Then Mark turned to a much nicer gravel road which led us to Wee Point resort, though my car stalled at the entrance gate and I could not restart it.

Thankfully, Randy had some connections in the auto parts field and in no time, got my car towed and fixed. The resort was not fancy, by any means, but it was charming, in a very rustic, sort of way. I enjoyed sitting in the Muskoka chairs and listening to the waves and the Robins, about twenty feet away from the front porch. We used to camp at Providence Bay on the island when we were young, and I remembered the caterpillars that hung from long web like strings from the trees, that got caught in my hair as I rode my bicycle. Those were here too, so I made sure to avoid them.

I was starting to feel like I had become an old lady before my time. I loved playing in the dirt, planting flowers, and watching the new bird tenant that moved into one of our bird houses. There were two swallows and I named them Sam and Ethel...see what I mean? This made me think of a Spanish poem that I had read, which said, in much nicer words, that you can't walk while gazing at the stars when you have a stone in your shoe.

(¡No puedes caminar, mirando las estrellas,
cuando tienes una piedra en tu zapato!)
Author unknown

Dad was helping us a lot with the patio and interlock project. He was so handy. He had the cinder blocks atop a ladder to add weight and had rope attached to either end to pull the ladder horizontally thereby leveling the dirt for the stones. So ingenious! It was really nice to be able to contribute financially and physically to these projects. I told Mark that I was just "coasting". I loved my life, where I was, what I'd done and of course my wonderful hubby and animals. I started to get the urge to start a family. Mark and I had accomplished everything in the right order, had good jobs and a nice home. We wanted to wait a couple of years after we got married to get debt free, before having kids. I also thought, it would be better to make sure that my job wasn't just a temporary position, as it was when I was hired. But, friends of ours started getting pregnant. We knew of three that coming year, and Mark's niece, Mary's eldest daughter, Valerie (same age as my sister), had just given birth to Calem on June 30th. I couldn't help the little envy, I'd been feeling. When she was pregnant, Valerie experienced the strangest thing while at College as she was walking down the school hallway. A fellow student approached her to share that she saw a likeness of an elderly man, describing her late Grandpa, Fred, and how she could see him and that he had his hand on Valerie's shoulder. This was very comforting for the family, knowing that Grandpa was likely watching over her, and her unborn child.

Dad was handy, and always thought preventatively. Mark was not mechanically inclined, and would get upset when things didn't go well. He was still trying to sell the boat. The bottom end of the boat had seized due to a broken seal, and had to get rebuilt. The first potential buyer came to see it, and it wouldn't start because of a defective water pump that Mark had bought for it. The second potential buyer had driven from Timmins to come and see it and wanted to see it in the water. Mark wanted to trade boat trailers, so that was a good opportunity to do so.

On the way to Ramsey Lake to show his Dad's boat. Mark took the guy for a cruise and ran out of gas in the middle of the lake. The guy decided not to buy it. When we got the boat on the trailer, the trailer had a flat tire. Then, I cut myself on the fender trying to tighten the bolts on the wheel. Mark was never a Beaver or a Cub Scout, and never learned to "be prepared". Mark had enough that day, and really felt like the Universe was against him.

We went to visit Mary's family in Sault Ste Marie. Mark had been in Chapleau the day before and I had to work, but was now off for three days, so we met at Mary and Romeo's. We went gambling at Kewadin, on the American side, as they seemed to pay better, and the drinks were free.

Work was going very well, but I found the night shifts were difficult. I wished I could have gone into a field so that I could look forward to Fridays, and have holidays off. I often had to leave early, or go to bed, when Mark had the neighbours over in the backyard around the campfire. At work, I encountered a new 'Crazy Corrie', by the name of 'Suzette'. Suzette would call in sick frequently, tell one part-timer that her Aunt just died, and the other that it was her Uncle. She got one part-timer in some hot water, and was terrible for gossip, to get the focus away from her. She played against my rules, and I judged her for it. I did not like her, and found a flaw to unions. It protected these people, that didn't seem to want to work.

Mark kept me sane, though. We spent our second wedding anniversary in Niagara Falls. We had four days off. We did a short wine tour, had a great dinner at "The Beef Baron" restaurant on Clifton Hill, and went to the new Niagara casino. I had a little too much to drink during the dinner which made me brave. So brave in fact, that I brought up the topic of starting a family. Mark would get uneasy when we spoke of children. We agreed that we both wanted kids, and discussed if it would be better to wait until we were more financially ready. He would say, "How much does it cost to raise a child?", because we had recently watched a documentary that talked about the cost of raising a child to the age of 18 was approximately $150 000, or more. By the end of our conversation, Mark said "If you win and are ahead by $150 at the casino tonight, we'll start trying to get pregnant."

Well, I did superbly well at Blackjack that night and left with more than $150 to the good! He encouraged me to keep playing, but I wasn't going to lose my good fortune. I think we shocked ourselves and I started getting cold feet. A couple of weeks later after some awkward intimate experiences, I said to Mark. "How about we don't try having kids until I've at least been working at the hospital for one year" (I had started in March). To that, he agreed and seemed to be more relaxed. Afterwards, it was announced that our Prime Minister, Jean Chrétien, would extend the maternity and parental leaves, to one year combined, with pay. Previously, it was six months paid, and two months without pay. This was to start in January 2001. We decided to start trying to conceive in March 2000. I would have been working for one year at the hospital, and would qualify for the year off. Mark took this seriously, and our bank contact laughed when I went in to sign the papers for our RRSP loan. She found it amusing at how Mark had the next three years planned, including of course my one year off. I felt so blessed to have such a wonderful man. He would be a great Dad!

There was such foreboding for the start of the new Millennium, and lucky me, I was working the nightshift. What was going to happen to the computer systems after the stroke of midnight? Absolutely nothing.

Mark took me out for lunch at a Chinese restaurant called "The Orient". He told me that I'd been more amorous and trying to get pregnant. He said it jokingly, but I thought he was right. I sure had 'babies' on the brain. He said that after the kids come, the only way we'd have sex would be if he bought me presents. That I'd have no more use for him after his mission was complete. What a joke, I thought! I hoped that we'd always have time for ourselves and hoped that with kids, that life could only get better!

Mark was on a boy's fishing trip one weekend, in May 2000, and my brother BJ was in town. Mom picked up Mel and I and we went to meet BJ at the Jem Mart convenience store, at the corner of Douglas and Regent street. As we drove up, none of us recognized him. I only suspected it was him, because he was the only one standing there. He gained a bit of weight, (6 feet tall, and 210 pounds), but he looked good. He had short hair, and was clean shaven. He hopped in Mom's car with us, and we headed to Tim Horton's for coffee. We gave him a hug, and started trying to get caught up. It was hard though, as five years had gone by since we had last seen him. I suggested that we go visit Dad. Everyone was game, though I wasn't sure how he would react to BJ. They had a lot of bad memories and a lot of regrets.

I'll never forget Dad's face, when they hugged. Dad wouldn't let him go, and his eyes welled up with tears. His face was red trying so hard to hold them back. A rogue sob escaped despite his efforts. The emotions spread like Dominoes from Dad to Mom, to Mel and I. It felt like a silent apology, then he said "I'm glad you're okay". I guess Dad may have expected Brian to be in a worse disposition. I caught him looking at BJ a few times, with eyes that were red and full of regret. I thought he really needed this, I thought we all did.

One night, Mark and I went for dinner at East Side Mario's, and he had a few drinks before we got there, and was little rambunctious but somehow was quite serious and sincere when the subject of kids came up again. This time he said he admitted he'd been thinking about it, and thought it would be really great, BUT, he made it clear that he would not be able to handle a child that was mentally or physically "challenged" or dependent for life. This made me cry. I was very disappointed with him. This is where we were very different, because I could handle it and would deal with whatever God gave me. The crunch was he believed strongly that it would strain our relationship. I was disappointed to hear him talk that way, but I know he spoke of how he felt and I hoped we would never have to cross that bridge.

Mel moved out to Mississauga, in Southern Ontario, to work as a Manager in training for the Shoe Company, and Dad announced that he and Renée were breaking up and he would be moving to Newfoundland. I thought Dad must be feeling lost, and I didn't want him to leave. We thought the world of Renée. She had a great sense of humour too, even during a trip down south with Dad when she got seasick and vomited her false teeth over the side of the boat. This was the beginning of their one week's vacation in a tropical destination. Dad pointed to a cemetery they passed in the bus on the way back from their excursion, and suggested they stop at that cemetery on the way back to the resort, to get a deal on some false teeth. We missed her after they broke up. The two things she left me with were the appreciation of Meditation, and a great "Au Jus" recipe.

Another month, and another period. I was looking forward to a break from my thirteen-day long, marathon periods, and they were heavy. It wasn't until a weekend where we laid more than just interlocking stones in our front driveway, that my wish was granted. I knew the next day, and the day after that, I just knew that something was different. Mom and I drove to Ottawa a week later, and we discussed baby names for real this time. I kept going back to the name "Abby". I'd always loved that name for a girl.

No sooner did we arrive in Ottawa and walk in the door to my Aunt Dianne and Uncle Rod's that my Aunt was having some emotional outburst and seemed to not even notice that we were there. As the minutes past, Mom and I looked at each other perceptively. Dianne had Alzheimer's, too. It was a bittersweet trip, and I don't think Mom discussed this with Rod while we were there. Were we the only ones who knew, because we spent so much time with Nan?

Mark lost his uncle Albert that year. He was a bachelor and never had any kids of his own. He lived alone on Lasalle Boulevard, and had been very close to Fred and Mark. He had slow growing prostate cancer that had spread to his bones, and two weeks before, he had said he had no pain, but his foot was bothering him, so he bought expensive orthotic slippers. The gun with which he shot himself was the very same gun that he had once taken away from his Father who after finding out he had cancer, threatened to do the same thing. Albert saw Fred suffer and I suppose he didn't want to get any worse. I hoped this wasn't in their genes.

Being pregnant was great, particularly in the second trimester. I felt like a superhero, and never got one cold. I felt a little change come over me, as now I had to do my best to care for this little one growing inside of me. The books said that it was okay to have sex during pregnancy, but I didn't enjoy it due to my restraint to ensure he didn't go too deep. As my belly grew, it was the most awkward exercise ever. There was no comfortable position for me and everything put pressure on my bladder which made me want to pee all of the time. So, this felt more like a wife's duty, than something I actually wanted to do. I just couldn't get my head around the panic associated with it. Mark came with me one weekend to the Labour and Delivery floor at the Sudbury General Hospital, we still called it that, but the name had just changed to St. Joseph's Health Center. We went to the labour and breathing class. I think Mark and I were surprised at all the jobs for the partner to make the contractions more tolerable for the mother. I liked the idea of him being there until the end, but I knew he'd be uncomfortable with seeing any blood or my insides, until it was over. For me, I needed the emotional support for the anticipated pain, but I also really looked forward to seeing Mark's reaction when he first would meet our baby and hold him or her in his arms. Mom also planned to be there too, which was a big comfort to me. I was hoping to get an epidural, as I wasn't planning to be anyone's hero.

I did get a cold in my thirty-third week of pregnancy. I had a little scare during my night shift, having thought my water had broken during a bowel movement. I was stressed about it. I went to St. Joe's in the morning, after my shift to get a screen for amniotic fluid, which was negative. I was monitored for an hour due to my elevated blood pressure. False alarm. I started feeling wobblier and walked in a side to side motion, and started feeling the night shifts very difficult. I had to sleep in our spare bed, as I flipped around all night like a slow-moving fish out of water, trying to find a comfortable position to sleep.

I finished work a few weeks before my due date, which alleviated the swollen ankles. I got some exercise at the mall, where I'd park at the opposite end of the food court and Dairy Queen, so that I'd have to walk back with my ice cream treat. The baby's heartbeat continued to be in the 150's through my third trimester, so I really had a sneaking suspicion that it would be a girl. I had a few instances of Braxton Hicks contractions, which were always a little alarming, and then one night, they really started. It was about 2:30 in the morning. I waited for a while then Mom came over, too. We went to the hospital around 8:30 am, and my contractions were pretty unproductive. They kept me there, had me walk, and kept checking to see if I had dilated. My water broke while I was there, and with each contraction by the end of the day, my cervix still had not dilated. They induced me by intravenous oxytocin, and the contractions were on top of each other and back to back, I could hardly catch my breath. Dad, Mark, Mom and Mel were there and were taking shifts to cool me down with a cool, wet, washcloth. The baby's heart-rate was also being monitored, and they could tell when I was about to have another contraction from the monitors display. Dad's facial expression showed alarm, each time they knew my contraction was about to start, and he was in the ready status. After I got the epidural, I hardly felt them. The needle was like the tiniest mosquito bite, but the heavenly peace that followed was most welcome. The next contraction after that, Dad was ready for, but I just closed my eyes and didn't feel it. I was able to rest. Amen! After a very long day, I had only dilated 1 cm. But the water had broken, which meant that the baby had to be delivered that day.

The nurses raced in when the baby's heart-rate was alarming, and it appeared that the umbilical cord was wrapped around the baby's neck. The heart rate would alarm through each contraction. They had to do an emergency Cesarean section. They upped the dose of my epidural, and I only felt the pressure and no pain. Mark was dressed in the surgeon scrubs, and had the little green hat, too. He came in and sat by my head while they operated behind a curtain placed just under my chest. Mark actually peaked over the curtain once, and didn't pass out. I'll never forget, the feeling when they cleaned the baby, checked her vitals and handed her to Mark.

It was the best moment to see him holding our baby. I was shaking violently, but still melted at the sight of them. She was healthy and perfect. She had brown hair and blue eyes. We called her Abby Kaitlyn. I had a little trouble with the breastfeeding at first, and the Doctor let me stay an extra day in hospital when he witnessed my sobbing frustration. I was so grateful for the lactation consultant who made Mark buy cabbage and refrigerate it. Alternating heat packs and cold cabbage in my bra, did wonders for the inflammation and engorgement. It had to be cold and crumpled to release the enzymes, and acted like a diuretic. I felt like She-Ra, the Princess of Power in the 80's Masters of the Universe cartoon. "For the Honour of Grayskull!". Finally, Abby was able to latch on, and I didn't have to give her formula. I wanted to do this right.

The first day home, Mark had rented 'The Blue-collar Comedy Tour'. I jokingly told him he was cruel, because the laughter was very painful on my abdomen, and it felt like my stitches were coming undone.

It was tricky in the beginning, as we weren't accustomed to the little sounds that Abby would make. I was so afraid, that she would stop breathing, or would choke while she slept. I got up frequently to check on her, but with major abdominal surgery, it was very painful. We learned to have some faith, and turn off the baby monitor at night. We could still hear her cry, and respond when she did, but didn't have to worry about the little noises. This was the only way, that we could get any sleep.

Change was inevitable. I never wanted to nag, but Mark was not always a believer in science and felt that certain 'rules' we're only created due to advertising or someone's financial benefit. He also told me to throw out my pregnancy and baby literature, as he thought it was making me paranoid.

Anytime I brought up a "they say", he would ask for proof. So, I avoided these conversations as best I could. He had a hard time with the baby stage and felt very awkward. He wasn't comfortable with the unstable head, of the baby, and he had a hard time getting close to me as I was always tired and always on duty. I found it was getting difficult to balance them both. Then when he was cuddling comfortably with Abby trying to get her to fall asleep, he would lick his finger and rub it in a downward motion from her little eyebrows down her eyelids, I was beside myself. He was attempting to make her eyelids heavy with his saliva, and all I kept thinking about was her clean little eyes and the microbes he was introducing. She never had eye infections so I didn't have the proof he needed to stop.

With lack of sleep, my brain function was operating in a deficit and I was very emotional. I wasn't comfortable with anyone but my parents holding Abby. They understood my expectations. Harriet had gotten a little shaky and weak, and her balance was not the best. I made sure to be close by when Abby was in her arms. She taught her how to wave. She usually just sat with her, which was best. Dad would come over, almost daily, as he was working at converting our garage to living space. He would bring me a coffee, and have some cuddle time with Abby and he'd pace with her nestled in to his forearms, facing him as he he sang to her. Sometimes he'd make up his own little ditty's, some I'd never heard before, and sometimes he'd sing "You are my Sunshine", like he did with us. He used to make Mom laugh, with the songs he would make up. He had a good way with babies, and they were comfortable in his strong, loving hands being lulled to his soft, hilarious tunes.

That year, Harriet went on a trip to Cancun, Mexico, and stayed at a condo that she rented with her friend Yvette, and Yvette's son and daughter-in-law. They had to prepare their own food that they bought from local grocery stores. One day, Harriet had a seizure and didn't know where she was. She had no history of epilepsy or previous seizures. She went to the hospital in Cancun. Betty called the hospital to find out if she was in any shape to fly home. We scrambled with the insurance company and had to purchase flights for all of them outright to fly her back to Canada together. Once back, she was definitely confused and not herself. We were very worried. She recovered somewhat but continued to have episodes of weakness. Her knees gave out when she was working in her garden and Dad was concerned, when he helped bring her to a chair.

I brought her to the emerge one day that she was getting worse and complained of blood in her stool. They admitted her, and checked her for enteric illnesses. They wanted to release her, but I refused to bring her home. I wrote a letter, and the nurses supported me, as she was getting worse in hospital, and could barely walk. Something else was going on, and they didn't want to investigate, as she'd only been admitted for the blood in her stool, not all of the other symptoms.

She passed away when Abby was one year old. We didn't make it before her last breath, as we were in Gogama, an hour and a half north of Sudbury, at a cottage with Abby. When we went to Harriet's wake, I pointed to her casket and said "That's Grandma", Abby waved goodbye. Grandma had taught her to wave, after all.

Life wasn't staying the same. Change was inevitable, and everyone that touched my life, changed me forever.

CHAPTER FIVE

The Price of Success

With my shift work and Mark's traveling out of town a couple of nights a week, daycare was very difficult. Most structured daycares only took kids for standard day shifts, and I was too nervous to leave Abby with just anyone. We found a few very nice people to fill in. Two caregivers worked out of their homes and one out of ours. When I was offered a temporary part-time job at the Public Health Laboratory for a little less pay and day shifts only, I jumped ship. It was a difficult time at this new lab. They had a small staff, their Senior Medical Laboratory Technologist had just been diagnosed with cervical cancer, and a temporary office staff had just been diagnosed with meningitis. Everyone was devastated for their coworkers and on edge for their own health. They went for prophylactic vaccines, just in case they had been exposed to meningococcal meningitis.

Another all-female environment. With some growing pains, I found my place, and I really loved having most weekends off. When I did work a weekend, it was mostly to just carry a pager that never rang, and to go into the lab to read the drinking water plates for Total Coliform and *E. coli* growth. This took only one to two hours in the beginning. On three-day weekends or Stat holidays, we had to stay a little longer to read the virus tube cultures. This took only from two to four hours. I missed some of the hospital work, but the lifestyle was worth it. I loved that Friday's meant the end of the work week.

Big things seemed to happen every three years. We were married after dating for three years, we had Abby after three years of marriage, and we had our second baby three years later.

In 2004, we gave birth to a boy. We had the "million-dollar family". This is what Harriet would have called it, when you have a child of each gender. We almost called him 'Charlie', as this is what Abby wanted to call him. Charlie was the name of Mark's late Uncle, and it was also Mark's second middle name, 'John Mark Charles'. Once I was in recovery, I said "Let's just call him, 'Charlie'", and Mark said, "No, he looks more like an 'Ian'". He had a similar nose and fingers to Abby, the 'Thomas nose', fingers like Harriet. He also had blue eyes, but his hair was fairer than Abby's, who had become a light brown. 'Ian Charles' he was named, after my Dad, and Mark. Ian was a much different baby than Abby, and it was a welcomed treat to be able to walk away from him in his crib at nap time. He just quietly fell asleep. That was amazing to me. When Abby was a baby, I had to use the little Tai Chi, which I learned at the YMCA gym, to get her into her crib without waking her. Abby was a good big sister to her little brother. She found him pretty funny, and she was a mini-me reciting rules to him. Ian adored his big sister. After a few months into maternity leave, I had palpitations, hair loss, anxiety and was about ten pounds below my normal weight. I even started thinking I was becoming diabetic as I didn't feel well after sugary treats. I had a moment one afternoon, that really made me understand a little more about mental illness. I was having thoughts and urges of hurting the children, but I had the strength to subdue and not act upon them. This scared me. The Doctor tried me on an antidepressant, which made my life worse. It didn't fix any other symptoms I was having, and made more tension between Mark and I because it completely numbed any potential orgasm. I had all the feelings leading up to it, then no fireworks, no surges, no release. So, I thought, if I had testicles, this is what "blue balls" would feel like! This made Mark feel like a failure.

One day, I was sitting on our bed, with baby Ian in front of me. I caught a glimpse of my reflection which made me do a double take. I had what looked like a donut elevated under the skin of my neck. I thought of 'Polkaroo', the costumed partner in the children's television series 'The Polka dot door', I watched as a young child. 'Polkaroo' had a long neck with a big colourful donut on its neck with a large giraffe like head balanced at the top. When I told my Doctor, he diagnosed me as having Hashimoto's thyroiditis. An underactive thyroid. Apparently, Nan had it, Aunt Dianne had it, and so did Mom! Life got so much better with a daily dose of Synthroid Levothyroxin.

Mark soon planned to take a leap himself with his career. Instead of being the District Manager, and travel, he planned to buy the furniture store in Espanola, an hour from Sudbury. He had a silent partner, Damian, to back him up. Together they bought a second store, this one in Lively, twenty minutes from Sudbury. A very expensive couple of years already, and this was the time that Mark's Uncle Roger and Aunt Jackie decided to sell their camp. Mark had always told them to let him be the first to know. One day, Damian and Margaret came up from the Muskoka's with friends of theirs, Cheryl and Lee. They wanted a winter destination, and went to Onaping to see Roger's camp. They came over for dinner afterwards, and proposed that we purchase Roger and Jackie's camp together, three ways. Cheryl and Lee owned a lumber business, down south. As our Southern Ontario friends only wanted camp as a winter destination, they planned to share the newer back cabin. We moved into the front, main cabin, which was where all of our wonderful memories took place when we'd stay with Jackie, Roger, Harriet and Fred.

Everyone loved it, and we were able to pay our third off gradually to Roger over a ten-year term. It made Mark sad though, that Roger and Jackie never visited us there. They had such great memories too, and I suppose they didn't want to see the changes made to the place.

Damian was crusty. He had white hair and always wore white shorts, commando, and stark white running shoes. His first wife forbade him from seeing his two biological children. The only children he knew children were Margaret's twins, that he helped in raising. Margaret worked with him at their furniture store in the Muskoka's. He lived by very strict rules, which obviously came from his father, and judged all who didn't align. He had a very big ego, but it was supported by his abilities. He could build or fix anything... for a price. He would buy boats or airplanes, fix them up and make a profit. He had money invested in apartment buildings, and real estate, and at least quadrupled the value of their waterfront home in the Muskoka's.

He had vision and the know-how to make things happen. Margaret inherited a green thumb from her father, and made the home a show home, with beautiful landscaping. They worked hard to get where they were. They had a beautiful home, but were more comfortable to hang out in their garage with their dogs. Damian didn't like many of the furniture sales representatives, but he took a liking to Mark. He often had him over, as Mark was the Company District Manager at the time. This was how they met.

With some renovations, the back camp became a cottage, with two bedrooms, and expanded a couple of times, for comfort. They built an additional outhouse, where you couldn't see the piles of excrement below, as it was more of an enclosed toilet. Fancy.

Damian and his friends rebuilt the front wall of our cabin, to change to the newer second-hand windows and location of the door. They also built a small two-piece bathroom, about the size of a closet, with a composting toilet. This was pure heaven, to not have to trek out into the cold, dark, outhouse, particularly in June and July when the blackflies and mosquitoes would carry you away.

Damian even installed a water filtration and UV system, so that we could drink the lake water. With my medical background, and my job at the Public Health Laboratory, I knew to make sure to test this regularly. I wasn't interested in getting Giardia or Beaver Fever. But Damian would drink straight lake water, and never had any issues, so when I presented that there was a significant bacterial count, it didn't faze him. I had to figure out how to clean the system and the lines without him. They kept their camp locked, so I could not clean the line that went to their camp. He didn't seem to like listening to women.

They bought a Pontoon for the camp, and started coming up for all seasons. They made a flag called "Camp Quaff", (Quaff means to drink excessively), and they were always ready to party. "Get 'er into ya!", Damian would say. He pushed everyone to drink, as you had a problem, if you didn't. He fit in well at the lake, and made many acquaintances. He met all of the people on the island, there were four properties, and the little island across from us with Larry and Mona. They partied and would be up in until the wee hours of morning, hooting and hollering. I often liked having the kids as my excuse to go to our camp early. I just couldn't afford to lose sleep, and wasn't able to drink much anymore, so I felt like a party-pooper. Mark didn't like that I didn't always stay out, but he managed to enjoy without me, and would be frisky when he got back to camp. If I was asleep, he would try in the morning despite the hangover. It always surprised me how he could muster the energy when he didn't feel well. Then he slept for another couple of hours afterwards. Once I was awake, I was up. I could not stay in bed, so I felt short changed on my sleep.

Camp was a wonderful environment for the kids to grow up in. Just to wake up there in the morning, was a reboot. We enjoyed teaching them to swim, to sauna, to fish, to hike and to chop wood. We played dice, painted rocks, and spent time together. We had no television service, except for a VHS for video tapes, and a DVD player for rainy or buggy days. For the most part, we were unplugged.

Our front cabin, was at the point of a mini-peninsula on the island, and we were maybe thirty feet from the water, surrounded by water on three sides of the camp. It was a lovely sound to wake up to. I'd often get up early, and bring coffee into the screened in porch adjoining our front porch, and write in my diary, or meditate.

One day, we were sitting on our front porch, having a visit with a camp neighbour, and the kids were at the little beach, not thirty feet downhill, from where we sat. They had their life jackets on, as I made them wear them all of the time outside, and their rubber boots, and they kept getting closer and closer to the water. I heard Abby laugh her little head off at her brother, and when I looked at them, I could see that two-year-old Ian was standing in about two feet of water, bent at a 90-degree angle, face down in the water. His life jacket was holding him in that position. I nearly sprained my ankle, and got to him before he took in any water. I scolded Abby, that that wasn't funny, he could have drowned! They continued to always wear life jackets, but I was even less relaxed about it, after that.

The businesses were doing well, with Mark at the helm. He was a good man, and people respected him. He even offered advice to Damian regarding treatment of his employees, as Damian had a lot of turnover and was hard on them. Mark inherited an all-woman staff in Espanola, and treated them well. He found the dynamic a little challenging some days.

We soon decided to move to the lake and buy a house with an unfinished, new addition. It was on Whitewater Lake, in Azilda, ten minutes west of Sudbury. The previous owners had beautiful plans for it, but ran out of money. In order to purchase it, we asked Dad if he'd be willing to move with us, and he could have an in-law-suite there, and it would make it more affordable for us. Dad had moved so many times until he started staying with us, that we didn't want him to feel uprooted again. He consented thinking he was helping us out. It was great having him around. Dad finished the apartment downstairs, and Mark's cousin Denis, whom the kids nicknamed "Buddha", worked at finishing the house for us. Mark's friend John, was looking for a house with his Mom, and purchased our house in Garson, but by the closing date, our house was not in move in condition. We had to stay with Mark's cousins Buddha and Lily's for a few months.

My sister, Melanie reunited one year with a boyfriend from high school while she was back home, and they started a long-distance relationship. Mason was living in Yellowknife, accumulating flight hours as a helicopter pilot and mechanic. Eventually, Mel moved there with him for a few years, and then moved south to Vernon, B.C. This is where they were married, in 2010. Everyone that could flew west for the ceremony. We didn't bring the kids, who were six and nine, and that was a bit of a problem for Mel and Mom. Mark said it was a long and expensive journey for two let alone four for one day, as it took three planes to get there, Sudbury to Toronto, Toronto to Vancouver, Vancouver to Kelowna. We had just brought the kids to a tropical holiday a few months prior. We left Abby and Ian in good hands, with cousins Lily and Denis, and travelled with just the grown-ups.

We stayed at a hotel in Kelowna. The same hotel at which Mom and Dad were staying. The morning of the wedding, Mel gave Mom and I tank tops with the words "Bridesmaid" and "Mother of the Bride", each letter in rhinestones. I wore mine when we went to get our hair done. Mel looked especially beautiful that day! We had a bit of a race, and only Mel could drive her standard vehicle. So, we laughed a lot, and made it back to get dressed and make our way via Limousine to the Elysium Gardens. It was a hot day, and the Limo's air conditioning seemed to be on the fritz. It was a bit of a trek down a dirt road, and then we passed through a gathering crowd of Sudbury family and friends and made our way to the main building. We had to get Mel and Dad and the procession lined up beyond the trellis. It was a beautiful location, which was lush with flowers and vegetation, and the isle leading to the stage with the Female Minister, was lined with pyramidal cedars. The scent of lilac brings me back to this moment. It was a beautiful ceremony, and it was just myself and Robyn, Mason's best man standing with the Bride and Groom. I wore a deep lavender dress that Mel had picked out, and I had altered. The colours were purple and green, and they were lovely. I wished Abby and Ian could have been there. The ceremony was fun, and I felt so bad that I sped through my speech. I was nervous and emotional. Many of us had wished the wedding would have been in Sudbury, as both Mel and Mason were from there, but this was beautiful. I was glad she had chosen what they wanted, as many attendees may not have visited, otherwise.

During one of our continental breakfasts, at the hotel, it was just Mom and I. I sensed some unease with her, and when prompted, Mom said to me: "Jan, Mark is an Alcoholic". I grew quickly defensive and went into denial, and resented being put in the middle of her and Mark. Sure, he drank regularly, but was functional during the day. He was not aggressive or abusive and didn't drink and drive. I figured she just had too sheltered a life, and because she never went out or socialized, she didn't have a proper concept of how much is too much. Nan used to interfere with Mom and Dad's relationship, and Mom and Nan would spend many Sunday's around the kitchen table with tears during their visits. Dad would always be gone out. I did not want to carry this burden and have this weighing me down. I thought I should tell Mark, as I didn't think Mom and Dad talked enough about problems back then, and he could make sense of it.

Mark was floored when I told him, and to my surprise, angry. I didn't expect this to hurt him as much as it did, and I immediately regretted mentioning it. He did not know how to react to Mom, and didn't want to speak to her again. This burden increased exponentially, and I didn't know how to get them to talk to each other. Mom wouldn't say anything more about the subject, which became an underground cold war, lasting many years, and I remained in the middle. This made me more conscious of Mark's drinking, and I found myself always making excuses or jokes about it.

After a few years, Cheryl and Lee decided that Onaping Lake was a too far to commute, and they sold their share of the camp between the two remaining couples. We had lots of good times at the camp together, and Abby loved Margaret and their German Shepherds. Abby had such love for dogs and created a small scrapbook with pictures of all of her favourite puppies. Damian really beautified the place, and made it very comfy.

Mark's business side, took advantage of another real estate opportunity. He was approached by an acquaintance that he met curling, named Troy, who owned some kind of real estate or contracting company, where he'd buy fixer uppers and flip them. The concept seduced Mark, and they bought a house in downtown Sudbury, with Mark's money. They then, bought two more, one at the South end on a lake, and one in Dowling. But, with Troy's business charges and scattered receipts, Mark started having less faith in the profitability of this partnership. He found out that Troy was stealing from him. This turned out to be a relentless source of stress and a stronger need to drown his sorrows with the golden nectar, Canadian Rye Whiskey and Pepsi or draft beer. Mark would stop at the local bar down the street appropriately named, "The Doghouse". He would stop there on his way home from work to create work contacts.

My journal entries became rather cyclical...

> *Mark seems detached, he doesn't pay attention to me. When he comes to bed early, he wants sex, but if I haven't had any attention that day, I'm not interested. He feels rejected, he either complains that something's wrong with me, because I'm never in the mood, or he storms out, or sleeps downstairs. I feel guilty the next day, and think I should either suck it up and just do it. Then I do, and I don't orgasm, or yawn, and don't feel like a long session, he feels rejected, I pray that I can fix it....*and the cycle continued.

With his increase in drinking, and avoidance of eye contact or smiling at me, I started feeling very insecure. Where had our friendship gone? I felt that anything I did say, would come out wrong or be misconstrued. Consequently, I often bit my tongue, and focused on the kids.

Sometimes, if I stayed in the same room as he was in for a length of time, he would initiate conversation. If I didn't, he'd be up all hours calling people from his past, and I'd strain to listen, to hear about what he had to say about our life. Sometimes it was heartwarming and reassuring, sometimes it saddened me that he couldn't talk to me like that, with a smile on his face. I'd catch him outside, or wandering around the house, and he'd be so deep in his thoughts, that his mouth was moving. He was talking, but to no one in particular. His brow always furrowed.

Mark would wake up and be out the door within fifteen minutes of waking, without a word. In the evenings, he would always make dinner. If I'd had a rough day, his was always worse. He spent more time talking to his voice recognition software on his Samsung cellphone, than listening to the kids or asking about me. He was messy, but he only noticed messes in the kitchen, and would get very disturbed by a cluttered countertop, or dishes not loaded properly in the dishwasher. No matter how hard I tried to imitate the way he loaded the dishwasher, it was always wrong, and he'd be forever fixing it. I joked that he was the 'Dish Nazi'. After supper, he would always have the TV on and sleep on the couch. I said he was watching the "Snooze". At night, I couldn't sleep with the television on, unless it had a sleep timer and would shut off in an hour. Mark couldn't sleep without the television on, and he preferred to have it on all night. We didn't do anything together anymore, and there were days, that we hardly spoke at all, other than discussing who would drive whom, and what groceries we needed. Even our birthdays and anniversaries, were almost forgotten, and we were lucky to get a birthday card, or a "Sorry, I forgot to get you a card... (Happy Birthday 'kiss'). I knew this was what my parents were like. I had to fix it...but, how? The couple of times that I approached the subject of his drinking, he quickly dismissed it as a non-issue. He said he didn't drink during day, he was under a lot of stress, and he needed it at night, to try to shake off the day. Besides, every one of our friends, neighbours etc.., drank too. I didn't have a leg to stand on. It was all in my head. I often questioned myself, due to the thyroid levels, and hormone levels, and what time of the month it was. Maybe it was me. One day, I talked to Dad about it, and he said, "Jan, he's always been this way". I supposed that 'I' had changed.

One night, in April 2013, Mark had stayed up late, and it was 3:00 a.m., and after a while of tossing and turning, the music that was still playing in the dining room was keeping me up. We had a loft bedroom and sound really traveled up from the main part of the house. I crept quietly downstairs, thinking he'd fallen asleep to turn the volume and the lights down, but he wasn't asleep. He was sitting in the entrance at our big orange comfy reading chair and ottoman, by the fireplace. He was so insulted that after I crawled back into bed, he stomped upstairs to see for himself how loud it was. Once he came to bed, I told him he could put the TV on for a while. As long as I knew the timer was on, and it would shut off in 1 hour, I could fall asleep too. Instead, he said something about how noisy I was in the morning while making lunches and getting the kids ready for school. I apologized but felt bitter that only 'his' sleep mattered!

The next week, I stopped in at 'All about Massage' to book the half-priced laser hair removal package for the armpits. The lady at check-in was 'Eva'. I hadn't seen her since I was nineteen, working at Zap's, when she combed my aura. I thought that very weird at the time. It was no surprise to learn that she worked part-time doing Reiki (a spiritual energy therapy). She mentioned that so many people are out of sorts and having Alzheimer-like symptoms due to this extra energy that has entered the earth "Do you feel that?", she asked. Before I left, she asked me if I married a good man, and I told her warmly and truthfully that I really did. I left thinking that she actually did have an 'aura' about her.

In October 2013, Mark took the kids to camp, and I had to work Saturday and would go up afterwards. When they left, I felt so empty.

I missed the chaos. I knew it was good for me to have alone time. I went to bed early and slept in, because our dog was gone too, and I didn't have to get up for our morning walk. I felt really happy on Saturday. I danced at work, was appreciating the beautiful weather and was looking forward to spending the weekend at camp with Mark and the kids. I even was flattered at the grocery store when some guy made an obvious second look and a glance at my wedding band. That was nice. I wish Mark would look at me like that. I sang all the way to camp but the mood was completely sabotaged by Mark's energy, with the feeling that I was more like a responsibility. I wish he could just look at me when we've been apart and smile warmly, genuinely seem happy to see me. My emotions were constantly teetering. I could sing one moment, then cry the next. My light energy was immediately extinguished.

Then I felt selfish. Mark expressed that he thought he was on the verge of a breakdown. He'd lost fifteen pounds from the stress of these extra house projects. He was in tears. He said he hadn't even dealt with our bills lately which was unlike him. I encouraged him to let me help with something. I told him let's tackle one thing at a time. Saturday, clean up the Dowling house. Sunday bills, and meet with a real estate agent to list the house in Dowling. The house downtown was rented and the house in the south end was his biggest concern. I told him that once it was closed in from the elements, to take the time to decide the best approach. He said that Troy had stolen the $40-45,000 that Mark had already put into it and Troy's wife's name was on the mortgage. He was scared we'd lose big on this one.

In my journal, I said that I would write what would make me happier, as opposed to what made me sad, this is what I wrote:

1. Waking up with Mark in bed with me
2. When I need a hug, to get 100 % reciprocated
3. Eye contact during conversations
4. To be treated like my opinion is valuable and not just another rant.

5. When Mark leaves the house, just let me know that he's leaving, instead of disappearing.
6. When a neighbour or friend calls to ask if they can bring something, that I've already been informed that we're having people over.
7. That when I shovel the driveway, I am appreciated rather than being told I was wasting energy as someone will come later with their truck, that I wasn't aware of.
8. The kids do their chores without me repeating myself until I have to punish them for not listening.
9. That Mark wants to spend time with me.
10. When Mark smiles at me.
11. When I have enough control to not have desserts
12. When Mom is positive.
13. When Dad speaks to Mark directly about house reno matters, instead of me as he doesn't listen to me...(sniff)! I'm failing at this.
14. To say things and not regret having said them.

I made some great friends in my neighbours. We even made a book club, called the 'Lakeside Book Buddies'. We were a group of twelve women who liked to read, but also liked to get together. It was nice to have my own friends! Some of us would go hiking, scrapbooking, knitting or go see a movie. One night we went to see the 4:20 showing of a sad movie called 'Orange County', followed by dinner at My Thai restaurant. One of my favourite restaurants.

During dinner, Dad called me to ask where the kids were. He was panicking as he said Mark and neighbour Bob were supposed to go to the Doghouse and the kids were supposed to stay home. This is also what I was told. Dad looked everywhere upstairs and I told him I would call Mark and call him back. When I called Mark, I told him that Dad called in a panic wondering where the kids are and Mark sounded drunk and he was denying that the kids were with him and that he didn't know where they were. After steaming a little and trying to tell him not to joke, I asked, "Seriously! Are they with you?". He finally let up but made me feel stupid for even asking. "Of course, they're with me!". My blood was boiling.

At one of our book club meetings, after having read a book by Eckhart Tolle about "The New Earth", and new way of thinking, I was talking about these books about rules, how we are so critical about everyone else, because of the rules we live by. I read the back of one of the potential books, which described, how some people just seem to have it all together, and most of the girls said that sounded like 'me'. If only they knew.

The next spring, we had a really fun night with the neighbours. We always did. Mark made the arrangements, on Friday night, and told me afterwards. It had become a running joke, how I was always the last to find out that we were having company. My first instinct was always panic, and clean like a maniac, before anyone arrived. Mark had been good for me in that respect, though, as if it weren't for him, I'd probably never have company as my house would never be clean enough. It was always a continual battle for me to let go of my programmed brain, and endure Mark's spontaneity. Mark always said, "they are here to spend time with us, not to check out how clean our house is!". I guess I didn't want, "Jan will be remembered for her clean house" on my tombstone, but preferred to be remembered as, "Jan will be remembered as a Loving Woman, Wife, Daughter, Mother, and Friend".

The next morning, I got up early with Charlie for our walk, after a very late bedtime. I walked again afterwards with Parisa as Mark and Nick were still sleeping. Nick was a single man from Espanola, that Mark had hired to do some renovations for us, and Nick enjoyed partying with our neighbours, so would ask to sleepover on occasion. Mark moped around all day with a hangover, while I played computer, organized some of his house flipping files, took the garbage out, but had to dig my way down the snow laden stairs from the back deck to the garage. Mark had just pulled a bunch of snow off of the solar panels from the garage roof and left the snow where it fell. I watched our Sunday night TV show "Once upon a time" with the kids and by 9:00 pm, we were all getting ready for bed. Mark was in our bed, diagonally across three quarters of our King-sized bed, it was an effort to find my space with pillows. I think he looked at me then almost as if he figured I was a lost cause not worth staying for, he turned the television off and went down to the basement family room. He often ended up there, but as he left I felt like I should have been more receptive. He probably wanted sex, but he'd had a few snoozes that day, and I was pooped. So, I felt guilty that I'd come across as cold and unreceptive. I felt so lonely. After a few minutes, I got out of bed and went downstairs to talk to Mark. I explained how I felt and what I needed and apologized for doubting his ability to take care of the cooking on Friday night when the gang was over, as he seemed too drunk. We discussed trying to spend more time together. He also brought up that I was too antisocial when I read so much during our trip to Punta Cana and that I hadn't made any efforts to seek intimacy. I had a good cry, but I felt like we had more of a direction. He came to bed.

In October 2014, Damian, our business and camp partner flew up to camp with his friend Jimmy. We arrived with the kids and Ian's friend, Eric. Friday was a nice evening. First thing Saturday morning, Damian stormed over and chewed Mark out up one side and down the other, accusing him of taking both of Damian's big propane tanks for the barbecue. His stance was very aggressive, and the kids could see the interaction through the big windows at the front of the camp. My memory is not the greatest and so I couldn't remember right off the top of my head, whether we had or not. Damian continued his rant, when Mark went over to his camp to talk to him about it, and explain that we did not have access to his camp and that my Dad brought us up a tank in July. I sort of remembered this, but didn't remember how we finished cooking when we figured out that we were originally out of propane. Mark wallowed in self-pity, and sulked and drank most of the day, and said how he didn't need this right now, with the amount of stress he'd had with the three houses. Damian and Jim left early that day. As we were sitting in the screened in porch later, I said to Mark that I think I may actually still have the texts in my phone from when we discussed the propane with Dad this summer, when Melanie and Griffin were up... and sure enough, I did.

Tues, Jul. 9 ,8:19 PM

(Me) *Oops! Out of propane. We should have a tank in the garage. Can u fill and bring also, tomorrow?*

Mark said we should send Damian a screenshot of this text. I apologized to Mark that I didn't say anything when Damian was angry, but I didn't remember. He said I should have said something. So, now I had the information, ammunition and the green light. I texted Damian, and copied Mark and Margaret on it and I included the screen shot.:

(Me) *Note the date of my texts with my Dad. You shouldn't have attacked Mark as you did yesterday. A big man would admit when he's wrong. My husband is not a liar. You really hurt him.*

(Damian) *I did not Attack him, I simply asked where my two extra propane bottles are. I keep extra propane and gas because we don't fly empty or full ever. Where are the empty tanks if I used them? I would admit if I used them. The empties would be there. I never called him a liar simply asked him, where are they??*

(Me) *Your tone was condescending and condemning. You absolutely were accusing. We don't have access to inside your camp, which is where you said one was. The other, maybe you brought it home. We never took it.*

(Damian) *There is two propane tanks at Mona's?*

(Me) *We don't go through THAT much propane*

(Damian) *K*

Amp for sale

Camp for Sale

(Me) *Mature.*

(Damian)*?*

(Me) "Camp for sale". Are you selling, because of this?
(Damian) *Yes, it is for sale*!
(Me) *How much?*
(Damian) *$125 000*

Mon, Sep 29, 7:51 PM

(Damian) *You are right A big man would admit when he is wrong!*

This was yet another blow to Mark. All of our money was tied up in these houses that he bought to try and flip, and they weren't selling. This meant no money to buy him out of the camp. We'd have to sell. This was a devastating thought.

Later Damian emailed Mark to say he'd be contacting the accountant about what the businesses we share are worth, as he wanted to sever ties there also... all over propane, or me calling him on his rude behaviour. A woman.

CHAPTER SIX

Hitting Bottom

In 2015, Mark was on the brink of a nervous breakdown. I really didn't think he could take much more. He called his friends Corbin and Peter. Peter used to own the Lively store with a partner. Peter stayed on as the accountant, and his partner worked at the store when Mark and Damian bought the furniture store from them. Mark hired Corbin, Peter's son, as the Manager and offered him a bonus percentage each year for the amount that the sales had increased over the previous year. They seemed to enjoy still being part of the family business and were definite assets to its success. They also became very dear friends to Mark, and said they would step up to the plate for Corbin to take Damian's place as partner. This was something that was in Mark's succession planning, but he wasn't expecting it to happen so soon.

Every night, Mark continued to sleep downstairs on the couch. He only came to bed when he wanted sex, and those nights were few and far between. We were supposed to spend Thanksgiving weekend at camp and have a nice big turkey dinner with Damian and Margaret. She made the best sausage stuffing. They were supposed to have their Thunder Bay friends come to camp to join us, but Damian set the course, and this was not going to happen this year. I was really angry with Damian. Mark had been more forgiving and was treading cautiously as he had more insight on the money we had at stake. Mark didn't want me to go to camp as he was worried I may make things worse. Sure, Damian helped us out, but Mark was always good to him and provided a very profitable business arrangement. What gave him the right to treat Mark the way he did? What really bothered me was what this was teaching Abby and Ian. "Don't stand up to a bully, when you are in the right"? "Grovel, instead"? So, I didn't go to camp. I had to work on Saturday anyway, but didn't go up after my shift as I normally would have.

Before the kids left with Mark, I reminded them not to get into a car or a boat when someone had been drinking and not to go with Dad visiting in the evenings as he would be drinking. This came up on Sunday, October 12, 2015. Mark was livid. I had to repeat two things when he called that morning, that he didn't remember already asking me the night before. Ian called me from camp, in tears. He had brought the phone into the camp bedroom to call me to tell me that Dad was really mad and he told me that he didn't want us to break up. I called back. Abby answered and I asked to speak to Mark. He started going on about Mason, my sister's husband, and how it was okay for him to drink, etc. I cut him off there and said it had nothing to do with Mason. It had to do with our kids being safe and making safe choices. He then said how in forty years, he hadn't had any problem. I reminded him that he had children, and had to think of their safety. My poor kids were now in the middle of this feud. I never wanted that. I remembered being in the middle when my parents were at odds. It was so very sad and scary for them.

In my journal, I wrote:

Was I wrong?

Was I not allowed to express my concerns?

Was I supposed to ignore the fact that Mark has a drinking problem?

It is so very hard to stay strong.

Happy Loneliest Thanksgiving weekend ever!

I'd just sent Mark this text:

10/12 9:34 PM

I think it's good, that the kids know not to get into a vehicle, when someone's been drinking. This is important for them. Please don't be mad about this, and understand. I love you. Goodnight."

While reading Eckhart Tolle's "A New Earth", I really started to see things a little differently. I told Mark that this book made me feel like he was the smartest man in the world. It described the constant chatter of one's ego that keeps one from living in the "Now". It really seemed to hit home for me. At the same time, I was reading "Rules of Life" by Richard Trenker and it had the opposite effect, and fueled the fire of being fed up by so many rules to live by and by which we judge others.

With all of this reading and trying to ignore my ego, and the incessant voice in my head, I still managed to kick Mark while he was down. After going back to bed after work, security monitoring called me at 7:00 am on a Sunday morning. Mark and I cuddled for a while as I tried to go back to sleep and he successfully slept (we had Dad's 71st birthday party the night before). Charlie, the dog, started showing interest in getting going for our regular morning walk.

As I started getting ready to go walking, Mark started getting amorous. I could never understand how he felt up to this when he had a hangover. I didn't want to stay in bed any longer. It was 8:00, two and half hours later than the dog usually gets out for his morning pee and poo. I ignored his advances, and took Charlie for our walk. Mark was cold and distant all day.

My ticked off ego thought of so many things to say but I kept a lid on it, until the kids finally went to bed. As we laid in bed, I turned to him said "Are you going to let me have it now? Why you were so angry and cold to me today?". I knew the answer before he even said it, which is probably why I didn't cry or feel overly emotional this time. That he felt rejected and that I kept shrugging off his advances.

It seemed that no matter how many times we had this conversation, he didn't hear a word I said. I told him that I preferred to be intimate in the evening after having spent time together or feeling wanted and loved. We were like roommates, living separate lives, and only coming together for sex when it suited him. I mentioned that day after day, he never looked at me, never smiled. I just needed some small display of affection, as he was never one to overuse the words "I love you".

I said that the only thing he wanted when he arrived home every day was a drink. The kids had been asking me about it and I kept trying to avoid the subject. Was this my ego? I knew I had the right to speak up, I was just worried that having done so, Mark would take as absolute rejection and not constructive criticism, on top of the business, the camp, and the house issues that he was juggling.

For the whole next day, Mark and I only texted. It was kind, and business-like. We had a very warm embrace when we got home from work, and he refrained noticeably from drinking. He felt more present and attentive all evening and I felt reassured.

Mark and I went on a trip to New Orleans with my friend, Fran and her husband Chris. I thought it would be great to have an 'adult' trip without the kids, but I came home feeling even more disconnected from him. He wanted to stay in bed all morning and party in the pubs in the afternoon and night. I spent most of my days sightseeing with our traveling partners, who were fellow morning people. On our way back to our hotel one night, Mark and I passed a sex toy shop and he really wanted to bring me in and find some gadget to help me to reach orgasm. I figured I had better find something or he would be disappointed, so I found an alien looking dildo apparatus, that had all kinds of settings, and vibration patterns. I wondered if it could result in numbness or something similar to white hands that drillers get... At first, I was a little intrigued, but accompanied by Mark's frustrated sighs and obvious disappointment, that shut things down for me in relation to this toy. He was a little too rough with it, as he wanted it to work, which made me uncomfortable. Maybe I needed to figure it out on my own, to avoid his frustration. How could anyone orgasm, knowing their partner is upset about it? Goodbye orgasm!

Before we got home, Abby left for her two-week placement as a Legislative Page at Queen's Park. She would stay with Lise, a colleague of mine who lived in Brampton and commuted to the laboratory across from Queen's Park. Lise was so accommodating and ensured that Abby got to her post and waited for her on her late days where she had to stay until 6:00 in the evening. I was so proud that Abby kept her head on straight and was so motivated. It was an honour to be chosen to apply, and an achievement to have her essay and application chosen. It was a wonderful experience for her. We enjoyed our face time through social media where she showed us where she was staying and she could see us and feel more connected. She asked us to save some of Grandpa's birthday cake for her. She grew a couple inches in those two weeks, as when I picked her up at the bus depot, she had grown taller than me.

Back home, our weekends were always filled. We had company almost every night, and often, Mark seemed like a zombie, present only in body. He only smiled when we had company. Every evening, Mark would be rubbing his lower legs. He had the most muscular legs, for someone that didn't exercise. He spent most of his work days standing on the cement floor. He got orthotics from his friend Rob, a chiropodist by trade, but this didn't help. He couldn't wear socks and shoes made him uncomfortable. I had put my Fitbit, step counter on him one day, and he didn't reach 3000 steps, compared to my 12 000 steps per day, on average. He had brown spots around his lower calves and hardly any hair left. We were thinking the spots were from blood pooling and he would mutter under his breath, "my legs, my legs, my legs". He showed them to everyone, and I encouraged him not to sit on the kitchen peninsula all of the time while watching television, letting his feet dangle over the edge. When he did sleep in our room, he often would sleep diagonally on the outer edge of our king-sized bed, with his legs hanging over the edge.

His nightly drinking resumed. At camp, one weekend he fell three times. One right after sex, it was dark, and our camp room was small. As soon as he stood up, he fell into our closet. Getting out of the boat at our neighbours at around 1:00 in the afternoon, he fell out of the boat, and then across the water at Mona's, he fell and this time got a black eye. I called him 'T-Rex', as I wondered why his hands hadn't saved his face when he fell. Each night after that seemed to get worse for his sleep, his demeanor and the pain. He would nap through the evening when he got home from the Doghouse, and would pace around the house, murmuring, or do laps around the pool table, downstairs because the pain and numbness in his legs and feet were unbearable.

After a few months of negotiations between Corbin and Damian, they came to an agreement and Corbin was also able to become Mark's partner with camp and the Espanola store.

Mark's stress was now as a result from the houses that he was renting. It was almost like, he was programmed to be in a constant state of stress and being a victim. I was so tired of making excuses to the kids and everyone else about him.

I was waking up. On our third annual Lakeside Book Buddies weekend getaway, in September, the girls drove almost three hours on a trip to Wasaga Beach. We stayed at the Saga Resort where we rented a cabin large enough to sleep eleven. Only six of the twelve Book Buddies could make it. Mom, Colette and Joanne were all retired, so they left early on the Friday and stopped to shop in Parry Sound, and Deanna, Monique and I left after work and met them at the resort. We arrived about an hour after the rest of them and went looking for a restaurant called "The Georgian Circle" which was known for their homestyle cooking. We had to make two U-turns to find it, having good laughs as we passed this phallic looking wooden totem structure on someone's front lawn. We were thankful for the MAPS navigation feature on the iPhone, that directed us to our destination. That is, once we turned it on. We enjoyed our dinner then returned to our cabin for wine, margaritas and a game of dice. There was so much room that we each got our own beds and Mom and I were the only ones with our own bedrooms. Mom snored like a trucker, so this was a good plan.

Before retiring for the night, we had agreed to hire this mobile massage therapist for the next afternoon for 30-minute massages for each of us. After breakfast, we were all very game for the 4 kilometre hike called the "Blueberry Trail". That is, until we noticed the sign at the entrance warning of the presence of the endangered and non-venomous "Hognose Snake". Consequently, we were four instead of six. Colette and Joanne decided to walk the beach boardwalk instead. We had a nice walk, with no snake sightings. It was a little on the cool side, but comfortable in the shelter of the trail. The leaves were not yet turning colour but there were no bugs, which is why we loved to hike in September. Our hike lasted only an hour, so we decided to check out the boardwalk next. It was very cool and breezy and closed for the season but we managed to walk and write in the beach sand.

We returned to the cabin to meet up with Colette and Joanne and enjoy sandwiches and Colette's homemade soup for lunch. We texted Linda from the mobile massage company, as she had wanted to come earlier than the scheduled 2:00 pm, if we were back in time from our hike. She showed up around 1:40 and before she started, she opened all of the doors that we had closed, and burned sage throughout the cabin. She then set up her portable massage chair in Mom's bedroom. We had figured amongst us, who would go in which order but Linda, when introducing herself and explaining the process said that she would decide the order. She had us fill in registration forms and explained that she was a Registered Massage Therapist, also trained as yoga instructor and Reiki energy work practitioner and claimed to also be a medium. In the end, only half of us got a massage. I was not one of them.

When I laid down on the bed, she asked me to move closer to the edge. I apologized and proceeded to move closer and she snapped at me that I'm always "sorry"! The cards and the spirits told her what treatment we would be receiving, and I was to get Reiki, and a visit from a loving spirit. She asked me who it could be. I thought mediums had more information to offer as far as a spirit's identity or appearance. I couldn't imagine if I were to believe her, who I knew and was close enough to, who would want to visit me from beyond. I said I wasn't sure, that maybe it could be my Grandmother (Nan, Mom's Mom). We were close, after all, but it had been many years since she'd passed away.

Linda told me that Nan was very proud of me. She also said that someone took my power from me and that something happened to me around seven years of age. I led a very sheltered life, so I couldn't imagine to what she was referring. We adopted BJ when I was eight, and that wasn't too problematic, until later. She applied pressure to my shoulder and to my hips and stomach, then put pressure on the inside of my knee looking for pain, and asked me if I felt a pulse. She asked me to relate to a colour, without thinking about it. I said "Purple". My current favourite colour. Then she asked me, "Where is Purple? Don't think!" A little confused by her question, and thinking of my childhood. I only remembered my bedroom being my favorite place, but it was pink... That reminded me of Alejandro once telling me I wasn't watching the news or educating myself enough about the world and told me that I can't stay in my pretty pink world forever. She asked me again who took my power from me. That I support everyone else, but not myself. What was getting my shoulders in such knots? I gave in, and decided to play along. I briefly considered telling her about my piano teacher, and how she would slap me if I didn't get the notes right, but instead, it seemed like the perfect opportunity to vent. I told her that I was worried about my husband's drinking. She said "That's it!", and "your Grandmother is showing me "lots of bottles"! Ok, this part, I was really not believing, but my concerns were real.

She told me for me and my children, I had to leave and go to Al-anon. An alcohol support group for families of alcoholics. She kept telling me that I need to leave him and I told her that I wouldn't leave, but would work through it.

She said she saw four children. Did I miscarry? No. Do I have Grandchildren? No, and thanks for the insult! And was I on my first or second marriage. First, and only one, hopefully. Looking back, I was one of three children, plus Mom had lost that one when I was about three years old, that would make four, wouldn't it?

She said she saw a fifth child, my inner child. And I had written all of those poems from the perspective of my inner child. She said that I was a 'Crystal Child', a child of light and they need more of me. And that is where it ended, with her fierce recommendations for attendance to Al-anon meetings, a support group for families living with an alcoholic, and that I would find Shiatsu massage beneficial.

I was dumbfounded when I left the room, changed into a swimsuit and headed for the hot tub to join Mom, Monique and Colette, and it was all I could think about.

After Linda left, we all got ready to watch "Wild", a book by Cheryl Strayed. We had read this book and found that it was made into a movie. I warmed up the meatballs, that I had prepared and we had supper, and played more dice. We didn't drink much and Mom went to bed by 7:00 as she was coming down with something. The rest of us stayed up until 11:00 then called it a night. It was a rainy morning and our stop to the Elmvale Flea Market on our way out was brief due to the poor attendance of vendors. We stopped to have lunch in Parry Sound. Had a good laugh when Mom hugged a tree on the sidewalk because Linda had told her to, then headed home. Mom went for chest x-ray a couple of days later to find she had pneumonia.

Just over a week after returning home, Mark followed Abby upstairs while I was having a bath. As he stomped after her, she was crying to me, and he was shouting "Don't defy me!". We had three laptops, one was Abby's for school as she was in the Laptop program, and the last time he used hers he had drained the battery and left many tabs open, which slowed her down considerably during class. I told her to put a password on it to discourage him from using hers. After I got out of the tub, and went up to Mark with the two other laptops in hand, he was sitting at the peninsula in the kitchen. I said "There is no need to use Abby's laptop, hers is for school, pick one of these". I motioned to the laptops as I heavily set them on the counter in front of him. "That was unacceptable how you reacted to her, and your drinking is starting to affect this family". So, I planned a family meeting. I discussed my concerns with the kids and told them I am not leaving. I explained that families need to fix their problems by talking about them.

Mark made an appointment to see his Family Doctor, but it was months away. I encouraged him to call to see if he could get in sooner or go the clinic, but he always made an excuse. He thought he was getting MS, or Fibromyalgia.

The Sunday morning that the kids and I decided would be best, I had all of us go downstairs, announcing to Mark that we were having a "Family Meeting". Mark didn't want to partake and mumbled disagreeably but he followed, eventually. I had forewarned the kids about the topics being covered and told them to bring forward their recent experiences or concerns if they were comfortable in doing so. I knew that this could be a family illness and wanted us to be open about it for the kids' future, too. When Ian felt the subject approaching, he ran out of the room. He sheepishly returned but was on the verge of tears and Abby was surprisingly strong throughout the process. She shared her recent experiences with her Dad's drinking. She brought up points such as: His using her laptop; his lack of memory for conversations from the night before; not being comfortable to ride with him in the boat, after he had been drinking. This resulted in his ensuing anger and impatience with them.

During our meeting, I got pretty teary and sometimes had a hard time getting the words out. He sat in the corner of the brown sectional couch. He listened and didn't say a word. At the end, we told him we wanted him to stop drinking for us. He didn't say anything.

We didn't see him upstairs for the rest of the day. He didn't come up to fill any drinks, though there was a bar down there. I actually believed that he wanted to prove that he didn't have a problem by not drinking for one day. The rest of the week he was withdrawn. He still drank, but it seemed to be less. Since that day, he plummeted. He couldn't sleep nights because his feet and legs were giving him such discomfort when he was at rest that he had to keep pacing. He had pain and numbness for weeks, and he had the shakes and a really rounded back as he paced through the house, alternating mumbles of curses and "my legs, my legs…".

He never came to bed. It seemed as though when he was home, he was on the brown sectional couch downstairs trying to sleep. He was finally rid of Troy, and we took a loss. But now he was having problems with the tenants at the houses he was renting. One, always late, the other separating and the third, needed new tenants. He had a Property Manager for the downtown property. He was having a hard time making it through each day and participating less each day, in home and family life. He no longer made supper, stopped grocery shopping, and had so much pain and numbness in his feet that he had a hard time driving all the way to Espanola (one-hour drive) without stopping along the way to rest his head and feet. He had received free basketball tickets to see the Toronto Raptors and took Ian. Ian sent me a text saying he was bored and sent pictures of

Daddy sleeping in the truck as he had pulled to the side of the road to rest. The staff at work and neighbours that popped in were growing concerned. He was always sleeping, and didn't look like he was taking any pride in his appearance. I continued to encourage him to get in earlier to see his Doctor, but he persisted that it wouldn't happen before December.

One day, I got a call at work from Corbin. He said he was bringing Mark to the Emergency Department. I thanked him, and told him I would meet him there, as it was next door to the Health Unit building where the Provincial Public Health Laboratory was located.

I went to pick up a pita sandwich for both of us, before heading to the hospital. Once I had arrived, I walked right into the consultation room to join him and the nurse. He was only talking about his legs, but I filled her ear with his drinking problems and our resulting family issues and stress from business issues the past summer. As a result, she ensured to include liver function tests. He paced until he was called to the next waiting room, and after about three hours we were called in to see an Emergency Doctor. She was young and I felt bad having the impression that she was a nurse. I filled her ear too, and she asked Mark if what I was saying was true, and he agreed. She said to him she wasn't sure if she could fix his legs that day, but would try to find out any physical causes but said there may be something going on mentally and would he agree to see a Psychiatrist. He consented. She told him his liver enzymes were high and he needed to stop drinking. We left with a note to go the crisis centre and she asked if we could go together, the next day. He had a rough night and didn't want to go the next morning.

Our neighbours brought over some herbal sleep aids for him, but he was going crazy with pain. Colette even drove him to work one day after his week off because he had to sign checks. Dad, the kids and I were worried and felt helpless.

He stopped drinking.

Finally, he had his appointment with Dr. Jeffries. The Doctor gave him pre-gabalin to help the numbness and pain in his feet, for the peripheral neuropathy, but didn't yet know the cause of it. He ordered three scans, an abdominal ultrasound, an X-ray and scan for his feet that was scheduled for May. Mark said that once the results come in, the Doctor would call him back for another appointment.

Mark started to feel so much relief from this medication. He started sleeping through the night and became more engaged with the family. The Emergency Room Doctor seemed to get through to him that his drinking was a serious problem and he had to stop. This seemed effective, as Mark started buying low alcohol beer, 0.5%. I was hopeful that life would get better.

I felt like I had been trying so hard to be strong for him and the kids and not talking about this with anyone, that I had many good cries. I was having a hard time coping. In the midst of his pain, in November, I had a Doctor's appointment as a follow up from my concussion from a curling fall in October. I wanted to discuss my concerns that maybe my thyroid level was too low as I had gained 5 pounds, was felt very emotional and had no libido. As I sat in the waiting room, on my scheduled day off, Mark sent me a text. "What time will you be home? Maybe we can cuddle?" I felt such a lump in my throat. I had my whole day planned with my Doctor's appointment, blood work and groceries and now I had to feel guilty on top of that because I had to make him feel rejected. Again. As soon as Dr. Sawkiw walked in and said, "How are you?". I couldn't get one word out comprehensively, for the sobbing. The floodgates just opened. He said "Take your time. Are you hurt?" He had such a soothing voice and a supportive demeanor, it seemed to just bring it all out. When my outburst subsided, I explained what had been going on with Mark and how I'd been feeling and that I had a concussion. He said to me "Do you know of any fifty-year-old's that have changed their ways?", and he asked me a few times if there was someone else. Of course not! He commended me on wanting to stick around, and said he could offer me some medication to help me to cope. I remembered how I felt the last time on those kinds of medications and figured that would just put the kibosh to any future libido. I didn't want to have to take meds in order to live with my husband. Besides, the last time, the problem was my thyroid. I told him I would start going to Al-anon. He ordered blood work, ECG and an MRI to make sure the concussion didn't cause any internal damage.

Mark felt better for Christmas and after New Year's, we were invited to a gathering at the new next door neighbours, Joel and Joanne. They gave Mark a Rye and Coke and he took it. I had even had his non-alcoholic beer chilling for him, but he was too embarrassed to bring it. Mark and Dad both left early after the first drink and I proceeded to drink a whole bottle of white wine. I was surprised that I didn't have a headache but had been suspecting preservatives in Canadian wines, and this was an Italian wine. I hadn't had a drink in a long time, and felt guilty for enjoying it. The lack of gatherings seemed to be getting to Mark as he lived for company, but he was too proud to tell them that he wasn't drinking.

His Doctor's office called to tell him that he missed his appointment. He told the secretary that he was not informed of the appointment, and was under the impression there was an urgency to see the Doctor upon receipt of the results. She checked with the Doctor and called him back. She told him that the Doctor said it would be fine to come in for Feb. 24. Mark's interpretation of this was that there was nothing wrong with the scans of his liver, and that he could start drinking again.

One Sunday, he was preparing supper half bent over, mumbling "my legs, my legs…" His eyes were glossy and Dad and I were concerned. Something had changed. Were his pills not working? Had he missed talking them? I asked him and also commented, "You look like you're drunk!", but I truly believed he wasn't back to drinking. Until, that is, Ian took a swig from Mark's diet Pepsi can and spat it out in the sink right away. I tried it too, and sure enough, it was mixed with Rye-Whiskey. I was so angry and disappointed. Ian was scared. "Please don't tell Dad, that I found out!". I went downstairs to the bar and drew a line on the almost full rye bottle and dated it

"2/2'. Mark stayed home the next day. I think it was a snow day for the kids. When I pulled in the driveway, he was walking home from the neighbours. The next morning ("4/2"), I looked at the 40-ounce bottle of rye, and it was only a fifth full. He drank it on a weekday. I showed him the bottle and tried to get through to him that I knew he had been drunk that Sunday, and that the drinking had been directly related to his leg pain. He expressed that the Doctors had been wrong before about his iron level, which was true, and that his results were fine and how could he just stop with the friendships he'd made? I told him I needed help. That I would start going to Al-anon meetings.

A Thursday afternoon in February, I took some vacation time, and left work early. I parked by Christ the King Church and walked up to the side door labeled 'Al-Anon', with a little poster. There were stairs going down and an open door to the left at the bottom of the stairs. As I made my way down, I felt a huge lump in my throat and it felt like my head was in a vice. Since my concussion, strong emotions really burned the temples and back of my head.

As I walked through the door, I noticed tables set up in a large rectangle, coat hanger to my left and a kitchenette to the right with coffee and tea available. There was a little, portable book shelf with flyers and a bin of related books. A few people, mostly elderly, were there chatting amongst themselves like this was their book club. I froze. A kind woman approached me, recognizing me as a newcomer, and she introduced herself. I couldn't speak, I started to sob and I just couldn't stop. She asked me if I needed a hug, and I nodded and let her hug me as I tried to catch my breath. The others gradually approached but not too quickly to say hello, and shake my hand. They all had a knowing gleam in their eyes and I found them comforting. For the meeting, they each took turns at being the lead, and reciting from a program book and then a few topics were brought forward, written on a piece of paper and passed around the table.

Each person could pass or discuss any or all of the items on the paper. I don't remember what the topics were and I was the second to receive them. I found my voice, introduced myself and gave a brief summation about my husband's recent health issues and how drinking was believed to be the cause. No one said anything, except "Thank you for sharing". As I listened to the others and to the initial messages that were recited, I realized a couple of things.

1) Others are in worse situations than we were.

2) Let go and Let God. Many of them have just learned to take care of themselves and stopped trying to change the loved one.

This gave me two choices: Leave or ignore the problem.

I couldn't do either of those things, so where did I fit in?

I left the meeting, feeling empowered by the thought that I didn't have to be the booze police, and letting go of that responsibility. But, I wanted him to know how we felt, and how this was affecting the rest of us.

One night, he said he felt like he's walking on eggshells and didn't know what to say.

He said he couldn't just stop drinking with all of the relationships he'd developed.

I told him, I would not police him, that he needed to talk to his Doctor. I told him it didn't matter about rules or what society says, last weekend he was drunk and complaining about his legs again. There was undoubtedly a direct relationship between drinking and his legs.

I relayed to the kids that the Doctor will have to tell him to stop drinking and that it is a disease. Ian approached me and asked me why I hadn't left Daddy yet. I told him, if Daddy had cancer, I would not abandon him. Alcoholism is a disease too, and I love him and won't abandon him for that.

Meanwhile, the tenants at two of the houses indicated that they might be leaving. The one in Dowling hadn't paid rent since November, and we had a restoration company and insurance involved in assessing the damage from a leaky roof. This just added more stress.

Mark had been drinking and hiding it. I could see it in his eyes and smell it on his breath. Another bottle of rum was empty, in the liquor cabinet.

I promised the kids a movie, one Saturday. That morning, I went downstairs to spend some time with Mark and he started to get frisky on the couch. I told him "tonight" as it was 10:00 in the morning and the kids or Dad could have walked in on us there. Besides, my period just finished, I needed a shower, but first I had to get some cleaning done. We were supposed to go to camp, but it was too cold. (-44° with the wind chill). Mark just laid around all day snoozing on and off, I did my chores, got cleaned up, had supper and got ready for some downtime with the kids to watch a movie. We started watching one at 8:30 pm. Mark seemed upset by this and went upstairs to our room. An hour later, he came down to see that we were still watching the movie and stormed up the stairs without saying a word. Shortly after, I heard the front door slam. The movie finished around 10:00 pm, and I went to bed. Mark was back and in bed, awake and emotional. He felt rejected. He blurted out that he walked to the Doghouse. I explained calmly to him that:

He knew I had said" tonight", and I was in bed by 10:00.

He knew we were going to watch a movie.

I didn't enjoy sex when it was daylight or the kids could walk in on us.

He was being unfair.

We hugged. He sobbed. Then we made love and I tried my hardest to shut my brain down.

He was in the mood again the next night. It was more passionate and it was Valentine's Day. He said "Let's go for dinner on Monday night", but I had a movie date with the girls already and planned to watch the movie, "How to be single." So, he suggested that we go instead on Tuesday night. We never made it out for dinner because the tenant from Dowling said he would stop by to pay or discuss his rent, but he never showed up.

By mid-February, Mark's sleeping patterns were getting worse again. My chiropractor asked me if I noticed any personality changes in myself due to the damage to my frontal lobe from the concussion. Interesting, I thought.

After work one night, I had to drive Abby from the Idylwylde curling practice to her friend Mia's in town for a sleepover. I got home to another little mess in the kitchen as Ian had stayed home. He remembered the night before that he was supposed to hand in his book report on "The Diary of a Wimpy Kid", which he read, but had now lost. It was due this past Tuesday and he had been given an extension. I let him stay home to work on it, but he was having a hard time remembering the story. No sooner did I walk in the door, that I got a text from Corbin, which read:

<Corbin> "Mark...I'm concerned"

I didn't want to give any information, Mark would be angry with me. I simply wrote:

<Me> "What are your observations?"

<Corbin> "Booze"

<Corbin> "Or he is upset about something I don't know but he is scaring me"

<Me> "I know, I'm in a support group. He's in denial, that alcohol is a problem. I believe it to be directly related to his legs. I'm hoping his Doctor gets through to him when he sees him on the twenty-fourth of February for his follow-up. Al-anon says to let it go, I'm finding that nearly impossible, as he has to come to terms with it. He needs to hear it from another source except me. He is hiding it in pop cans now."

<Corbin> "If it's alright with you, I would like to give it a shot. My issue is he may be upset with me for a bit but at this point I think it has to be done to save our relationship and our business. What do you think?"

<Me> "I think he has a lot of respect for you, and I would appreciate it too. He's ashamed and afraid that if he stops drinking he will lose all of his friendships. Thanks Corbin sorry to drag you into this!"

<Corbin> "No problem. My life is because of Mark so I will do what has to be done."

I put the rainbow trout back in the fridge that he had left on the counter to thaw and started making dinner for Ian and I. We ate by candlelight, just the two of us. Just after we finished eating (6:30), we got a telephone call from Chester's wife, Sheila. Chester was a friend and work associate of Mark's in Espanola. She called to tell me that Chester brought Mark home and left his car at the store and that he was drunk. I asked her if he had any other symptoms as he'd been to the emerge in November. She said, "he's just drunk" and she would get him to drink water and eat. I thanked her for calling as I was starting to worry when he hadn't arrived home yet. He had told me that he was supposed to meet the tenant from the South end, that night, so I expected him to be a little late. He wouldn't be coming home until the next day.

Mark got home in the afternoon and startled me as I was washing the walls of our master bathroom. The only thing he said, was "Did you call Corbin?". I said "No", because I hadn't, he 'texted' me, but I was not sharing that. That Sunday, Mark mentioned that he would be going to Corbin's house in the afternoon. The kids and I knew that this might be an emotional evening for him. I kept busy and made a couple of new recipes, a roasted cauliflower risotto and mushroom and parmesan stuffed chicken with rosemary from the Pampered Chef cards that came with my new Rock Crock pot. When Mark got home, he didn't seem overly upset, just a little quiet and after supper, seemed to only be drinking cans of the PC Blonde Brew, a 0.5% beer.

The next evening was Monday. Before I went to Zumba, we sat together at the peninsula and I brought up the subject of the unanswered text that I sent him earlier that day. "Do you want me to go to your Doctor's appointment with you on Wednesday?". He said "I'll be fine.". I told him not to hold back and to be open with the Doctor. He looked at me and said, "Don't worry, I'll fix this.". He slept really well that night, he said. I had a bath after Zumba, took a magnesium supplement a rooibos tea and curled up in our king-sized bed with my cuddly puppy. Tonight, Mark was supposed to be meeting with the tenant in Dowling to find out his plans as he still hadn't paid rent. It was going on five months of supporting this family.

Mark went alone to his appointment with Dr. Jeffries to find out about his scans. He said that Dr. Jeffries discussed and prodded about the psychological follow up and was satisfied by the crisis centre screening. He also recommended that Mark drink with moderation as his tests didn't show any problems with his liver. He told me this in the kitchen and I felt the heat rise along the back of my neck and the vice grip to my temples. I told him that I was relieved that the results were good, but I said the alcohol was still a problem and that it could not continue the way it had been. I told him I did not want to retire and watch him drink all day every day. He apologized for not making the best choices this year, and I told him the drinking has been going on for years. He seemed to want to hurt back and said that my comment to Damian this summer could have bankrupted us. I brought up his attitude the other night where he stormed out because I was watching a movie with the kids and not running upstairs for sex at 8:30 pm. He never wanted to spend time with me in any other way. He said that I never make the effort. I told him, the only way I'd ever be forward was under the influence of alcohol as it was not my nature. I told him I am not attracted to him when he's drinking and he's turning me off of alcohol. He promised to fix this, whatever that meant to him. We cuddled, without sex, for the next couple of nights.

Mark went to camp one weekend, and I had to work. The kids did not want to join him. When I moved the decorative pillows off of our bed, I found an 8.5 x 11inch white page with a heart drawn and "JMCT + JAD" written in the heart. That was a little teasing glimpse that the man I married was still in there.

CHAPTER SEVEN

It Takes a Neighbourhood

I started going every week for either massage or chiropractic adjustment and I dove into my hobbies. I made a custom jewelry and repair business and named it 'Bijangles'. The name was derived from "bijoux", French for jewelry, "bangles", for bracelets, my specialty, and "Jan", to personalize it. I went to Zumba and did my focused breathing meditation, though blocking out all the background chatter was nearly impossible. In the back of my mind, I often heard my Mom's words "Only you can look after yourself". With all of this 'me time', I continued to get marathon headaches that would last two to three days, and sometimes four. I figured this must be a side effect of my concussion.

Mark regressed into his old habits, and lived like a hermit in the family room. He drank whiskey or vodka from pop bottles, and was very secretive. He always looked disheveled and glassy eyed.

He wore the same clothes, and started to smell. He didn't eat much, and the bills were piling up.

I sent a Facebook message to his eldest sister, Mary, to say he needed a sisterly ear, and briefed her that drinking had become an issue. She called him the following Sunday. He was very brief. The conversation was not long and he said very little. The following weekend, on Saturday morning, Mark came into the laundry room where I was folding laundry and he was shaky, unkempt, and looked like he had an eye infection in his right eye. He said he had to go into work, and that his sister Betty and her husband Philippe were coming for dinner that night. I had taken two packages of chicken wings out of the freezer but he said he would pick something up at the grocery store on his way back from work. And off he went.

I was busy that day with house cleaning, and laundry, and decided to have a bath afterwards, to sink right back into the hot water and let it dissolve the increased tightening in my shoulders and neck. I felt another headache emerging. Once I dried my hair and got dressed, I stayed upstairs in our master bedroom to put away laundry. Mark, Betty and Philippe all arrived at the same time around 3:00 p.m. Betty had not been well and had been in hospital again with pneumonia. When she was sick, she was also quite secretive. She had many issues, and neuropathy in her hands and feet, that she said was due to diabetes, but that she also had another rare neurological condition.

Mark hadn't brought home any groceries, and I started to panic but he said we would try out the new pizza shop, in Azilda. Mark was surprisingly lively. Betty and Philippe had brought in some soft herbed cheese and crackers, and we had pepperettes and a hot appetizer that they picked up at Costco, to tide us over until it was time to pick up the pizza and wings for Ian, who did not like cheese. I wondered how Mark had transformed from that morning. Mark drank from his plastic bottle of Diet Pepsi, and by the end of the pizza dinner, he was falling asleep at the table. Diagonally across from him, Betty appeared to be doing the same, though this was more common for her and she wasn't a drinker. Often her eyes would be closed and she would appear to be sleeping, but she would hear everything that was going on around her and comment now and then. This day, I wondered if there was something else going on with Mark, other than the drinking. Philippe, Dad and I tried to carry on a conversation, and when I made a comment about something running in the family, Betty defensively awoke and blurted out that it was NOT the same.

They didn't stay late and I saw them off at the front door, and waved goodbye. Once I climbed the stairs to our bedroom, I saw Mark was semi-sitting on the floor in the master bathroom. He appeared to be in some distress. I rushed into the bathroom asking if he had fallen. He mumbled that he had and as I leaned in close to help him, found him to be sitting in a very large puddle of urine. I helped him up and out of his wet clothes and he murmured that he didn't understand what was happening to him. I was calm but firm with him. I told him it is his drinking, and he needs to stop. It is reacting with his pre-gabalin, neuropathy medication to make him a zombie.

This wasn't enough of a wake-up call for him. I recalled my Doctor's words when I broke down in front of him during my appointment, "What fifty-year-old have you known to change their ways?".

I never really saw much of him, as he continued with his daily routine. He would "sleep" or pace all night in the family room, mumbling about his legs, and then would leave for work while I was out walking the dog, so that I would not see him in the morning. Upon his return from work, instead of preparing supper like his old self, he'd be fast asleep on the couch, when I got home, or arrive late then go downstairs. Our conversations became scarce and I tried to keep positive for the sake of the kids, but they were suffering just as much as I was.

I kept reminding them, and myself, that this was a disease.

It was just too hot to sleep and my two-day headache had escalated to a migraine and I could feel my stomach threatening every now and again depending on my position to let my stomach contents re-acquaint themselves with my tongue. I had been awake since 2:00, so I texted my Manager, Doreen, that my headache was too much to bear and I would not make it to work that day. She texted back "Ok. Take it easy." So, I made sure Ian was going to get out of bed for school and it took everything to walk Charlie for his morning purge and could hardly lift my feet as I solemnly made my way around the morning fifteen-minute circuit. As soon as we returned, the kids were well on their way with their morning routines, and I made myself a nice cold blueberry spinach smoothie, rubbed peppermint essential oil at the nape of my neck and grabbed an ice pack for the top of my head and sat in my rocking chair in our bedroom upstairs to sip my smoothie. On normal days, Mark would have been long gone by now. But, he was late this morning. When he reached the top of the stairs and saw me on the rocking chair with the eye mask covering my eyes and the ice pack on my head, he mumbled "Meditating?". If I was meditating, I would not have answered, but I said "No, just trying to drink my smoothie". He didn't say anything more until he was out of the bathroom and asked if I was staying home today. I told him that I was staying home. I never made eye contact or saw what kind of state he was in that morning. I slept on and off that morning. It was sunny and beautiful and Dad was trying to fix the grease nipple on the ride on lawn mower outside.

At 12:45, I received a text from Corbin which read "Can we talk?". Everything tightened in my neck and shoulders as I anticipated this conversation. I replied "Yes. I'm home with a migraine. I can talk this afternoon, at your convenience." I warmed up some broccoli soup that I had made for Abby (her favourite) as I thought I should eat before Corbin called. I sat at the patio table in the shade to get some fresh air and talk to Dad a bit while I had my soup. No sooner did I bring my bowl in that my cell phone rang with a picture of Mark showing up as the caller. It was his cell phone, but it was not Mark on the other end of the line. It was Lisa from his store in Espanola.

She sounded calm, yet concerned and said "Jan. I'm sending Mark home but my husband Dean will be driving him home in Mark's truck." She said she blew up at Mark because she had enough with his pain, walking barefoot at the store every day. "He needs Detox", she said. He had been caught drinking at work and she told me that if he didn't get cleaned up she would leave. She didn't want to see him back for one to two months. I thanked her and told her that I really needed him to hit bottom and that he needed someone else, other than me to knock some sense into him. I thanked her again, trying to hold back the imminent sob and the burning at the base of my skull which I started getting in response to emotional stress. I disconnected the phone and hung my head and asked myself, "Now, what do I do?" I needed guidance.

I knew I had just under an hour to make some decisions and plans. Something had to be done, and I had to be the one to do it. This is the day, that time stood still. I felt every second, every heartbeat, as it pounded at my temples. I grabbed a couple of Ibuprofen, downed a glass of cold water, and got myself ready. I blamed his Doctor but thought maybe he could redeem himself and I called the office to hear the message "the office will be closed for…<click>". I hung up. I needed to think about what services were available for 'addictions'. We had visited the crisis centre, there was also OATC clinic... I was trying to think of clinics I had seen on patient requisitions coming through Public Health. I googled "OATC" and found the contact number, but tried four times as I tried to get cleaned up, and dressed.

Finally, someone picked up the phone, it was now 2:20 and they close at 3:00. Mark would be an hour away and not due before 2:30. Once I mentioned to the lady at OATC that this was in regards to an alcohol addiction, she stopped me and said this clinic was for other drug addictions, not alcohol. She helpfully provided me with two more options. The detox centre and the crisis centre. I first called the detox number and spoke to a kind gentleman's voice that confirmed this would be suitable for our situation and to pack him a bag for 3-5 days. After the call, I ran to find a bag and started filling it with his favourite t-shirts, lounge pants, socks, underwear, reading glasses, toothbrush, toothpaste, deodorant, electrical shaver and cell phone charger. I put the bag and a coat in the trunk of the car, out of sight. I told Dad what was happening and he was so supportive but worried about me. I started boiling water for tea.

I quickly unplugged the kettle and ran outside to intercept as I saw the truck pull in the driveway. I grabbed my purse and slipped on my shoes in record time. Dean stayed in the truck on his phone, as Mark slowly climbed down from the passenger side. I grabbed his arm in mine and brought him around to beside Dean to urge him into our car. He was swaying on his feet, but his arms moved quite abruptly in protest that he didn't want to get into the car. He tried to get his bearings by standing still, but his face was bewildered and frustrated. I tried to be firm and tell him that we were going to see a Doctor, that he needed to climb into the car. Dad appeared at my side. Dad was in tears, which I think scared Mark all the more. Dad placed his hand on Mark's back and said, "Please Mark, get in the car with Jan." Dad had to tuck Mark's right foot that continued to protest to the outside of the car, and I moved as quickly as I could to get the car started and locked the doors. My adrenaline kept me forward. I felt like every muscle in my body was contracting simultaneously and I was in high alert. I felt every breath, I heard every sound. All I could see was red. I was angry, I was scared, I didn't want to speak. He kept murmuring that this is all because of me, that I wouldn't stop bugging him. This fueled my anger, but I didn't speak a word. I kept telling myself, that he doesn't mean what he is saying. This is just the alcohol. Mark and I hardly spoke, except for him asking twice where we were going. I told him "to a clinic, the fastest way we could see a Doctor." He said that he didn't even have a drink today, it was 2:30, I hoped not, but his body language suggested otherwise. He mumbled, blaming me for this situation saying that if I would just stop "beating him up". I bit my lip, and pressed my foot a touch harder, on the gas pedal.

I had a hard time locating the 'Withdrawal Management Services' and had to drive by a couple of times before following a suspicion about a side street riddled with potholes and passing between apartment buildings which continued around to the back. There was parking and another building with a French radio station on the nearest side and the Detox center on the far end. I managed to park and have Mark get out of the car, however, he insisted on putting something in the trunk, his jacket. I hoped that in his state he wouldn't notice the full weekender bag.

I parked the car, not far from the entrance, and somehow managed to get Mark to the front door. In the foyer there was another door to buzz in. Two men came to greet us, when I said "Hi, we are here to see a Doctor". There was a young man dressed very casually, and another man in his fifty's that spoke to us, but all he said was "Say your goodbyes".

At this, Mark turned on his heel to leave. There was no way, he was letting me leave him here. I turned apologetically to the men, and said that hopefully, we'd be back. I followed him to the cement retaining wall to the left of the parking lot, where he was walking. He turned to me when I touched his arm but would not look in my eyes. I pleaded with him to just listen to me. I told him that he needed to give this a chance as there would be people to talk to, to find out what the problem was. I told him he could continue to blame me, but I wasn't making this up. It was obviously a problem as his friends and acquaintances were concerned and calling me. This needed to stop.

He was so angry, he could hardly get any words out. I don't know if he heard anything that I said. He walked the other way, past our parked car and toward the way we had come in. I stayed sitting on the cement retaining wall opposite the entrance, as he strode towards the car. His gait was far from stable, he was full of emotion, and the position of his shoulders gave him the look of defeat. I did not chase after him. I watched Mark try the car door, and then gave up with a huff, and walk away. I thought, "He'll think about what I said and he'll come back here, he knows where it is now". He had his wallet, but no keys and no cellphone. I considered chasing after him, but figured with no cellphone, he would come back. I would wait. I must have waited ten minutes. I considered leaving, but then worried that he was in such a state, he might not remember how to get back here.

I texted Corbin:

My text to Corbin: "I brought him to detox and he walked away. I'm hoping he comes back to the entrance. I'll sit here and wait".

And after a few minutes;

My text to Dad: "He walked away. He has no phone. I stayed at the entrance to talk to him. He doesn't have his phone. I'm leaving him to roam. He knows he needs to come here, maybe he'll think about it then admit himself. I'm driving home."

I climbed into the car and as I started driving slowly away, I replayed the scenario in my head and wondered, if I should drop his bag off, in case he comes back, then decided they would just have to call me for it.

I took the back roads, Pine Street, which runs parallel to Elm which leads to Highway 35 to Azilda, and then turned onto Ethelbert, to reach Elm. Just as I approached the intersection, I spotted Mark. He had just reached the same intersection on foot, and was crossing in front of me. I felt my heart in my throat when I saw him. He was now walking, as if he had a spear in one side. He was bent at a 45-degree angle sideways, and looked like every step was a huge effort. I parked the car, and raced towards him. He was livid, and almost looked like his eyes were not obeying his command as they bulged out of sync. His face was white, and I was worried that he would have a stroke. I tried to put the video on my camera and record his gait, instead I only captured the following conversation.

Me> "The kids can't see you like this, you need to fix it."

Me> "Come on, let's go to the hospital."

Mark> "No. No hospital."

Me> "You have to go to the hospital."

Mark> "No. I'm not going to the hospital."

Me> "Yes."

Mark> "No. I'm not." He bent over to catch his breath, hands on his knees.

Me> "If it's me beating you up, you know what? When we go home, I'm going to keep doing it! It's going to be the exact same thing, nothing will change. I'm going to keep harping about the drinking. It's going to be an issue for me.

So, let's go to the hospital because you're really suffering both physically and mentally. Everybody at work is worried about you, the neighbours are worried about you, and the kids. I don't know how long they can take seeing you like this. Come on. I need my husband back."

Mark> "I want to go home."

Me> "We'll go to the hospital, then we'll go home."

Mark> "No. I want to go home."

Me> "Please, Mark!"

Mark> "No. I'm going home."

Me> "Come on, get into the car..." Mark turned and staggered away. Then he pivoted.

Mark> "Give me my phone and I'll call for a cab."

Me> "No. Get in the car." I walked around to the front of the car. "Come on. Get in the car."

He staggered away, bent awkwardly to the right at the oddest of angles, and headed down Highway 35 West, towards Azilda. My head was in a vice grip.

I stayed in the car for a few minutes, waiting to see if he'd return. I knew he couldn't get far in the shape that he was in. As I waited, I texted Corbin:

Me> "He's refusing to go to the hospital, and wants to walk home. Look at him! "(I attempted to text a video of him walking, but it didn't turn out). "Maybe I can take you up on your offer to pick him up. He's walking home from downtown."

After composing the text and my nerves which were all firing simultaneously, I took a deep breath, and turned onto Elm St. I was planning to pull to the side and watch him from a distance, but as I drove, and drove, and scanned the side of the road and the ditch, I could not see him. "Someone had to have picked him up and given him a lift home". I thought to myself. So, I picked up the pace, making sure to go no more than 15 km/h over the speed limit and I called Corbin at work, but he had already left. I called his cell phone and told him to meet me at the house instead as Mark was no longer walking on the highway.

It was now after 3:00 pm. Abby would be home from school. I wished that the kids wouldn't be at home to witness this. Once I pulled in the driveway, Dad was sweeping beside the house. The neighbours to our left saw my state and asked if I was alright. I just shook my head "No", and beelined it to Dad who received me in a big emotional hug. Once I caught my breath, between sobs, I asked Dad if Mark was home. He said that he hadn't seen him. Abby was on the front porch and I asked her to look in the house for Dad. When she returned from a futile search, I informed her of what had transpired that day. I texted Corbin, who was just checking the Doghouse, Mark's favourite watering hole, and told him that I was going to bring Dad with me to walk the highway. I was panicking with the thought that he could be in a ditch having a stroke or some kind of episode, alone.

I said "Abby, you stay here, and call me as soon as Dad gets here."

I drove for maybe five minutes, when Abby called. We were just passing by Day Construction and made a turn-around at the next side turn off. I called Corbin and he said he had just pulled into our driveway "do you want me to go in or wait for you?", he asked. I told him it would be good for him to go first, and give me a few minutes to calm down.

Once we got home, Ian was already home, eyes as wide as saucers wondering what was going on. I asked that Dad accompany me downstairs to where Mark and Corbin were and for the kids to stay upstairs. I could hear Ian sob, and Abby's voice trying to explain the situation to her brother, as we made our way downstairs. Mark was in his regular position on the couch with the TV on, and Corbin was sitting on the opposite side of the sectional, arms on his knees and hands clasped, trying to talk to Mark. It was a very mellow atmosphere, a little somber with the blinds drawn and no light other that from the window opposite the side of the room and the glow of the television.

I took the lead and reiterated what I had said earlier, though this time, I said he could not stay here tonight. That was not an option. He had to choose between Detox and the Hospital. I reminded him that it was not just a problem with me anymore, neighbours and co-workers were concerned. Corbin piped in a few times, to give credibility to my speech and said it was a good idea and that he would hold the fort at work and Dad said, "Come on Mark, take my hand". Dad was trying so hard to stifle the emotion which was so intense that Mark recoiled like prey. He sputtered a few times, "I'll quit", but was not agreeing to leave his safe zone on the couch. Finally, something in him grew too tired to resist any longer and he consented to going to detox. I asked Dad and Corbin to come with us because I did not want a repeat performance from earlier that afternoon. Corbin walked with Mark and Dad and I walked together upstairs. I whispered to the kids that I would be back soon, that we were going to get Dad some help. We got his shoes on and got him as far as the car, then he said he needed me to open the trunk. He grabbed his tan brown denim jacket, holding it tight to his chest, like a baby in a bundle and walked back into the house and downstairs. Dad and I exchanged looks and I said "Now what?". Corbin followed Mark back into the house, down the stairs through the bathroom into the furnace room, where Mark stashed the brown jacket. They returned after what felt like an eternity but in real time was likely five minutes. And finally, Mark was in the front passenger seat and Dad and Corbin folded their long legs into the back seat of our red Dodge Charger. It was a warm, sunny afternoon, so I boosted the

Air Conditioner to try to keep them comfortable in the back seat. Mark didn't say much but Dad and Corbin made small talk as they tried adjusting the temperature controls in the back of the center console which prompted me to ask if they were too hot. In fact, I was freezing them out, to which we had a little chuckle, and I was grateful for a temporary break in the charged atmosphere.

This time, after about a ten-minute drive, I knew exactly where I was going and parked in the same spot as earlier. We brought Mark's bag and he had a sweatshirt that he said would suffice and made our way to the entrance. The same two men came to receive us and the one had said earlier to, "Say your goodbyes", said "Brought reinforcements, this time?", followed by, "Okay, say your goodbyes." I felt considerable anger and frustration towards Mark at this point so I had no problem making my goodbye brief and not too emotional. Corbin and Dad gave him a vote of confidence and we made our way out the door. I made sure he had his cell phone, but they said he wouldn't be able to use it while he was there and I was given a business card with the Detox telephone number.

The relief that I felt at that moment was reminiscent of the peace I felt when my brother left, years before. This was the right move. I felt it in every cell of my body. I felt strong.

Upon returning home, I talked with the kids and Ian said he wanted to tell the neighbours with me. I mentioned this would be wise as we were going to need their support if we were going to help Dad succeed in this.

Our first stop was to Bob and Colette's, a couple of doors down. We went there before supper and they had some knowledge that this was an issue around Christmas, and this past week I had been bending Colette's ear on the matter. In fact, they shared that our other close neighbours were gearing up for their own approach to an intervention. His problem was really so evident to everyone around him. He wasn't kidding anyone.

That night Ian helped me to pack up all of the alcohol and bring it to the neighbours garage to have it out of reach. We found a bottle wrapped up in his jacket that he had stashed in the furnace room and confiscated that too.

Many of the neighbours were in the backyard next door, and Dad was there too, helping remove some of the tree tops of the wayward trees with a man-lift and a wood chipper. I made my way without Ian, to talk to them and ask for their support in not offering Mark any alcoholic beverages when we get together. They were very understanding and supportive and confirmed that Mark would not lose their friendship because of this. I explained that this was his biggest roadblock to letting go of alcohol as many of his friendships nurtured a drinking environment. It really felt as though a weight had been lifted from my shoulders.

Abby kept herself occupied with her homework and her group video chats on social media. She was so calm and I kept this conversation as open as I could to invite her to feel that she could work through it in talking about it. She shared but she did not dwell. She understood that this was the right thing. Her biggest concern was how Dad would react after her outburst upon his return, as she had yelled at him and dumped some alcohol down the drain.

Mark called before bed twice that evening after 9:00 pm. His voice was more like his work, daytime voice. He sounded calm and thoughtful. He asked me to bring him reading glasses. I mentioned that I had packed them and that they were in the firm glasses case so he thanked me and said goodnight. He called again about seven minutes later to say that he found his glasses but could I bring him his gray jogging pants as the blue ones had bleach stains on them. He said, "If not tomorrow, the next day would be fine.". I let out a big exhale of relief that he was really going to give this a chance. I didn't tell him that I was not going to work the next day, and was keeping the kids home from school. We all needed some psychological mending from the previous day.

I called to change his Electromyogram (EMG) foot scan that was schedule for May, and went to the municipal tax office to figure out balances owing for the camp, house and three rental properties and sent our late income tax documents to the accountant.

As I was driving out of the underground parking lot of Tom Davies' square, Mark called again to say it was okay to leave for the appointment the next day. I told him I had changed the appointment but would call to inquire. He also asked that I bring Diet Pepsi, and a couple of big bottles so that he could share. I should have known he would have a party there too. I grinned inwardly and wondered if he could really change.

I didn't call the hospital to change the appointment. After hanging up with him, I considered it briefly until I remembered the challenge I had, in my first attempt at dropping him off, alone. As it re-played in the back of my mind, I thought, "If I pick him up for that appointment, there's no way in Hell, he would consent to return to detox. Best he stays there.

I finished my errands, picked up the Diet Pepsi and brought him his things.

After ringing, I heard a man's voice approaching, explaining that "we don't normally allow this", and there he was with his chaperone from the day before to greet me and inspect the bag I was delivering. Mark was shaking steadily. His eyes were glassy, and he looked a little unkempt, yet calm. I gave him a hug, but couldn't say much for the lump in my throat. I informed him and his chaperone that I thought it best that he stays and go to the new appointment for the EMG test for his feet, which I rescheduled for August. I made him a little uncomfortable when I asked for his cell phone to record the text conversations between him and Felix, our non-paying tenant for the upcoming hearing and explained that Al, his friend and lawyer would help us with the hearing. Mark quivered and swallowed hard and said "let's just call Felix and give him his money back." I knew I didn't want to get into this discussion now. "No. We'll go through the hearing process.", I then said goodbye and took my leave.

I was feeling a little angrier with him and more determined to get things ready for our hearing. Especially, after completing the forms a second time and bringing them to the Landlord and Tenant Board office, where they informed me that this had not already been done. Mark had lied and not dropped them off initially. All of this waiting for a hearing, and the paperwork had never been submitted! So, I expedited the request and got a concrete hearing date.

Mom came over for dinner that night. We were supposed to go out for our birthday dinner but in lieu of recent events, chose her coming over to talk and support me and the kids.

Mom felt guilty that she was scheduled to leave in a few days on her trip to Scotland, England and Wales.

It was a nice evening. Dad joined us also. He said we had been invited next door with the neighbours who were feeding everyone for helping with the tree clean up, but I told Dad we needed some family time instead. He agreed, and joined us.

On his third day at Detox, Mark had talked with a Doctor who prescribed a beta-blocker to help reduce his alcohol cravings and a requisition for blood work. He wanted to get a more long-term picture of Mark's blood sugar with the Hemoglobin A1c test as he suspected that diabetes may be attributing to the neuropathy in his legs. Mark wanted me to pick him up, so I told him I would be there by 5:30, after having taken the city bus with Abby to show her how to get to her RHP Training Centre. I had to walk back to my car, which I had parked at Gloria's Restaurant, then pick up the pictures of the rental house taken by the Restoration Company that we hired through insurance to assess water damage claimed by the tenant. Then I had to return to RHP Training Centre for 5:00 to pick up our daughter.

I had also contacted a couple of roofing companies in that time, and I met with the assistant at the Lawyer's office to explain our case and discuss that I was still concerned that the source of the leak may not have been identified. The restoration company said it was from inadequate insulation in the roof and ice back up, but I wanted to fix the roof too.

I picked up some non-alcoholic drinks from Your Independent Grocer. We pulled up to the Detox Centre by 5:35 p.m., to find Mark standing outside with his bag. Abby hopped into the back seat, disappointed that she would have to give up her favorite seat in the front.

It was a little awkward when we got home. The kids were trying hard to act normal and ask Mark what it was like at the Detox centre. He was brief in his responses and didn't want to share very much. We ate our spaghetti and meatballs in an uncomfortable silence, as we tried not to be too obvious as we watched Mark.

Mark stayed upstairs longer than normal and had a little rest on the living room couch on the main floor. We loaded the bar fridge downstairs with PC blonde and red 0.5% beer and cans of pop and flavoured drinks. He asked where the alcohol was, as he wanted to bring a bottle of the Port to Lisa at work. After trying hard not to disclose and telling him there was no hurry for that, I did cave and told him that I had brought everything to Bob and Colette. I hoped he wouldn't pester them.

Mark had some books and paperwork, and it wasn't until the next day that I heard the best news yet. He had met someone from Alcoholics Anonymous (AA), and was going to meetings. Every day, Mark's shakes grew weaker. He decided to go back to work the following Monday. He worried that if he stayed at home any longer, he would go stir crazy. I warned Lisa that day as she hadn't wanted to see him again before one month.

I was most impressed at how his daily reading in his AA literature had become his priority. It was a little juggle as he would work late, eat fast then head to the next meeting.

It was great when he was willing to share as I often tried to initiate conversation about what he was going through for the kids to see how hard he was trying.

One day, he mentioned that he was moved by a daily reading passage that he highlighted it in yellow and book marked it with a yellow sticky note naming it "weeds". How recovery was like a garden, with new weeds popping up that need constant attention. I thought, "He's really doing this!" and I felt so very proud of him.

I battled the urge to argue with him and resorted instead to tears as he was trying to make emotional decisions and wouldn't listen to me. For example, Jordie, the tenant from our property in the South end dropped off his rent to Mark at our house, and I overheard their conversation, which I had to discuss with Mark after Jordie left. Mark was trying to arrange for Jordie, a contractor by trade, to agree to move from the Hannah Lake to the house in Dowling, where the non-paying tenants were residing. He proposed to have cheaper rent while he did the needed work. The insurance company and First General Restoration company had done the assessment and we had received a check to start the work, and planned to re-assess if further work was needed once the drywall was removed. "Not again!", smoldered in my thoughts. I was so frustrated. The feeling had become so predictable, starting as a mound in my chest then burning the back of my skull. I said "No, Mark. You made this mistake twice before, it's just prolonging the inevitable." Plus, the non-paying tenant was still at the Dowling house until at least our hearing with Landlord & Tenant Board on May 31st. It was going on six months of no rent, from the Dowling property.

I was trying so hard to listen to the rules now set by the Lawyer's assistant. Get Insurance report, get three roof estimates, plus I got all pictures taken at the assessment on a CD. I had to make several reminder calls with the three roofing companies to ensure these estimates would be ready for the hearing.

One day, he was upset as he figured that I had sent the wrong tax estimate for taxes paid on what I thought to be the mortgage payments for the Hannah house. It was the one for our own house, instead. I had asked him before but he was overwhelmed and couldn't help me. Our accounts had been his project and not mine. How was I to know that of the two credit lines and two mortgages on the Bank account, the credit line was a mortgage? He snapped at me when he called up the bank accounts and showed me which one I should have sent to the accountant for our taxes. I asked "Why are you so angry with me? I'm doing my best!", and my eyes welled with tears threatening to roll down my cheeks. I wouldn't let them. He said what he usually would say when he couldn't justify himself, "I had a rough night, last night." I expected that this would be a roller coaster ride but I could not help being affected by it just the same.

He brought it up after work when I tried acting like nothing had happened. He said, "I know you were upset earlier. They said recovery sometimes affects you mentally. Some people go crazy." Maybe they were referring to some people's 'wives', I thought...

CHAPTER EIGHT

Power Reclamation

With my Dad promising to keep an eye on things, Abby and I were able to take our much-deserved birthday shopping trip to Brampton. Ever since Abby worked as a Page at Queen's Park for the Provincial Government, we made it our birthday trip every May to go birthday shopping and visit Lise and Terry, her billet parents. We had a wonderfully relaxing trip, and found some great finds. She was such a good co-pilot, travel companion and frugal shopper.

A couple of weeks later, I travelled alone to see my sister, her husband and my nephew. They lived in the Okanagan Valley in British Columbia. While I was waiting in the Sudbury airport, I read some pages from "The Power of Now" by Eckhart Tolle. It helped remind me to let go of worry about the past and savour every minute of this trip. I had a few wonderfully peaceful moments about the clouds sitting at the window seat and a nice, quiet, gentlemen sitting next to me. I didn't feel like making conversation, though had it in my head to partake at any opening.

I was happy though, to take the time to just be. At the Toronto Pearson Airport, I had a nice period of time of at least two hours to saunter to gate D39 and then backtrack to find some breakfast. I chose to sit in a restaurant and patted myself on the back for eating alone, which was one of my goals on my list toward stepping out of my comfort zone. I had an expensive BLT on a very crumbly croissant and read my e-reader like everyone else around me. I practiced looking inwardly to become aware of my breathing, my blood flow, and my extremities and at the same time conscious of the blurred conversation between a couple of gentlemen who seemed to be work associates, sitting at the next table over, all dressed up in suits. They sounded so formal, and it didn't sound like a comfortable experience. I fought my instinctive thoughts of judgement that surfaced.

To stop judging means to stop expecting others to live by your rules. Letting go. One thing that spoke to me in the "Power of Now" was a statement of one's choices which in summary rang familiar with Al-Anons' recommendations of leaving the alcoholic or "let go and let God". But what sounded so in tune to my current path is that this book shed light on a third option. That of *'change'*. That is what I wanted, that was my focus in every moment of every day. To appreciate and love the good, and to change the bad. I hoped that I would feel more deeply connected for the journey. It gave me warmth and hope to imagine once past this hurdle, that maybe Mark and I would feel closer, our love more infallible after surviving this difficult time.

I was a little confused at the Vancouver airport, as far as how much time I had for my next flight, but it was longer than I thought. I had time to buy some tea leaves at David's Tea and a decaffeinated caramel macchiato and cookie from Starbuck's. While I enjoyed my snack, I journaled a little about this journey. The plane to Kelowna was small like the one between Sudbury and Toronto. After a smooth landing, I walked down the seemingly endless Hallway to find my sister, Mel. I was so happy to see her, that

I fought back the tears of joy. What a roller coaster ride, I had been on!

My sister Melanie (Mel), made it her priority to spoil me and help me to relax. She had been reading the autobiography that I started to write on Google Docs, as I attempted to deal and sort out the events of my life, so she knew better than most how I needed this vacation!

We started our visit with a big hug, a silly double selfie, and sent it to the family to say that I had arrived safe and sound. Our first stop was at a local vineyard for some wine tasting, we had less than one glass each. Then we picked up my nephew, Griffin, at preschool. He was excited, yet apprehensive, as he recognized me from pictures and Facetime but it had been a couple of years since we had seen each other, in person. We went for a lovely Italian meal at one of their favourite local Mom and Pop restaurants in Vernon, called "Titas". Mel and Mason urged me to stay up as long as possible to help with the three-hour time change, but by 8:30, I succumbed, and went to bed.

Mel and I brought Griffin to preschool the next morning, then Mel dropped me off at a trailer park, to see her "energy worker" friend for a ninety minutes session. I kept an open mind, and really had to stay mindful to witness and explain what was happening physically in response to her hand pressure when she asked. I felt very relaxed afterwards and a little confused by what had occurred.

After lunch at an Indian buffet, we picked up some groceries for the boys' dinner. We prepared the vegetables and chicken and got our bag packed for our night out. Mel had taken advantage of the Mother's Day special at the Sparkling Hill resort and Spa. This deal included a three-course dinner, a night at the spa, use of the facilities and complimentary breakfast. We had each booked a ninety-minute facial for the next morning. We had a beautiful room, meant more for couples with two Queen sized beds to the right, and to the left, a glassed-in shower and a tub at the far window. We were relieved to have a door to the toilet. Flushing the toilet felt like playing the slots. The toilet would only flush when it felt like it, so we had to lift the back of the unit to pull the chain to get it to purge. Before going to dinner, we had time to call home. I spoke to Ian for a bit but he had his friend Ryan over, and we had to join skype to speak to Abby. This was a good way to show her our room. We had a glass of white wine, a Gewurztraminer (Gwertz), and snacked on chocolate covered acai and blueberries and trail mix.

We regretted our snacking as we had filled up before our three-course meal. We shared crab cakes and muscles in a coconut cream sauce and arctic char and beef tenderloin and dessert was delicious but just way too much!

We had a latte and waddled back to our room to get our bathing suits on.

We put on the white, terry cloth housecoats and slippers provided, grabbed the towels and room keys and went to the spa area to enjoy the dry saunas, the steam saunas, the infinity pool, hot and cold foot circuit pool and hot tub.

The spoiling continued the next day. We went for our free breakfast buffet, then to the pool and then made our way for our facials. It was very relaxing and the esthetician picked and squeezed and plucked and iced and massaged. It was nice to get a shoulder, neck and head massage out of it too! As I was leaving, she gave me a checklist of about six products that she figured I needed for my daily cleansing routine. She had used these three coloured test solutions to find that my face was in need of lipids and water.

I'd just started trying the oil cleansing method, and thought it a really good idea considering her analysis. We took our time and made our way back to the room to pack our things and check out. What a great start to my vacation!

Other than getting to spend some quality and much needed time with my sister's family, we also fit in some other activities. We went to a rodeo in the pouring rain, we went to the very impressive

Vernon Farmer's market, we shopped in Kelowna, and finally topped it off with a boat ride in the beautiful Okanagan Valley.

Mel was an excellent massage therapist, but she was also my crazy-lovable sister. She insisted that she was also treating me to a massage at her office, so we walked there together one morning after bringing Griffin to preschool. She introduced me to her office mates and went to prepare the room. She came pretending to be formal, but then quickly returned to her silly self. She did insist that since we were sisters, that I should trust her, and go ahead and take off all of my clothes, undies included. I usually keep my undies on, so this was definitely a step out of my comfort zone. Mom and I were more private than Mel was. But, I listened to my little (big) sister. She was taller and stronger than I was. She spent an hour and a half trying to fix me. She started on my abdominal muscles, another first and yanked my leg, and tried to physically adjust my hips, and shoulder, as they were curving in. She impressed me. She even worked on the fascia of my scalp, which was stuck after my falling on the ice and concussion. She also recommended that I stop wearing such tight bras, as I told her that I had lumpy breasts. She recommended self-massage to reduce the build-up of toxins, that can't be cleared by the lymph system. I left tender but I didn't have the constant shoulder-neck twinge that seemed to be my constant companion.

Afterwards, we walked to a nearby coffee shop called the Bean Scene. I had a chai rooibos latte that was simply decadent. We shared a chocolate ginger cookie too, as we sat at a little table in the patio behind the restaurant, in a courtyard atmosphere. We then walked, and shopped downtown. We walked home to get the car to pick up Griffin from preschool. As soon as we walked in, we saw him playing goalie in the gym. He was wearing his Teenage Mutant Ninja Turtle outfit which was actually PJs, and looked pretty intense in his hockey game. The boys were all playing hockey, the girls were dragging themselves along the floor pretending to be puppy dogs. One of them had a purple leg cast from colliding once with Griffin on a tricycle. We stayed to watch him for a bit, as he was not ready to leave, then we headed to the grocery store, to pick up some supplies for a picnic for the boat ride planned for later. The Okanagan was beautiful, and the homes on the water had elevators embedded in the mountain, for water access. Griffin and Mason did a little fishing. It was a lovely end to my restful adventure.

When I returned home, I noticed that Dad had ensured that the yard was well maintained. The decks were freshly stained. The house numbers were now obvious, as he painted them a bright yellow colour to contrast the brown house. He had also planted the garden. Mark and the kids survived my absence but the inside of the house needed much tending.

***

The hearing to evict Felix, was quickly approaching. The night before, I spoke to Mark again about the property in Dowling, and I told him he would be upset with himself later, if we didn't take care of the required renovations and roof before selling it. He still just wanted to sell it as it was. I told him I wanted to spend the extra $5000 and fix the roof and he acted like he did each time that I gave my opinion, that he couldn't handle this right now. I said "No. You keep giving your opinion only and closing the door when I have something to say. I will take care of the renos and the roof. This is what I want to do. I just need your consent." He somewhat acquiesced to the roof needing to be fixed before winter, which was enough for me to decide to proceed.

I did a little housekeeping on Saturday, but seeing Dad out by the lake that morning made me want to join him, to enjoy the moment. He seemed to have figured out how to be more present and enjoyed the quiet moments alone by the lake. I considered getting busy with the vacuum but I thought, Dad was getting older, and I should make myself a rooibos tea and go be present with him.

As I approached, he had received advanced notice as the dog had beat me there. I pulled up a lawn chair to sit with Dad on our narrow dock, from which he was fishing. He had to keep casting and reeling in as our lake was deeper than usual but was still only three to four feet deep at our end. It was a beautiful, calm, sunny morning.

We sat for a while on the Muskoka chairs and chatted and then chose to go for a paddle boat ride. This paddle boat had seen better days as Dad had to fix it a few times. Mark tried to give it away without asking us in the past and I stopped him. It was our only toy for getting out on the lake and it was lovely.

Dad and I paddled, and Charlie road in the back, then the middle, and then on the front of the boat. It was nice to go out as Whitewater Lake was usually quite windy and choppy but that morning, it was calm.

On the next day, I sat with Dad on a lawn chair under the willow and there were tons of large, almost beetle-like insects crawling everywhere. The more we stared at the grass, the more of them we could see. There were also dragonflies, one on each dandelion, at the base of each flower. We began to suspect that these insects were the dragonflies and we saved a couple, stuck within the mesh of the fire pit and one that Dad had picked up and put back in the grass, but couldn't seem to get its legs working to bring it to higher ground. Then as we slowly made our way to the house we spotted a dragonfly pulling itself out of its bug costume onto a dandelion and we both felt awed to witness this transformation. I said "Dad. We'd better not mow the lawn for a couple of days so these dragonflies can dry their wings out and take flight." I think that from now on, Dragonflies will remind me of this moment with Dad, and how I was transforming too.

As the Dragon Flies

Instinctively, I find my way to a tall dandelion
which has just gone to seed.
I grasp the stem and pull myself out from this nymphal shell.
I molt from this burden and stretch as my length allows.
My wings dry in the breeze, they lighten and slip apart.
Then I spread them to their full splendor.

Alan, our Lawyer, called me at work to confirm that he would meet us at the hearing the next day. I was relieved that he confirmed his attendance, because the Lawyer's assistant had advised me that Al hadn't been to work for the preceding week due to kidney stones. The night before, Mark had an Alcoholics Anonymous meeting and I needed to make sure all of our evidence was in order for the hearing. I was pumped, but nervous too. I thought of a few more relevant documents and didn't get to bed until after 11:00. Ian was disappointed as I told him he had to understand that I didn't have time to tuck him in. Once in bed, I should have meditated. I was antsy. Mark was too. He slept downstairs. I watched the clock until after 1:30 am. I kept talking to myself. "Calm down. You will be less nervous if you're rested. This is the day we've been waiting for. This is the thing that will fix Mark's stress. He will see how rules can sometimes work in your favour." I managed a few winks before dawn but I awoke before the duck quacking alarm on Abby's phone signaled 6:30.

Mark didn't sleep well either, and I could feel his anxiety. I thought of a couple more things to bring as evidence such as if it was mould, what kind it was, and the chances of it being a health concern. I dove into my Clinical Microbiology textbooks and the internet. My evidence folder was two inches thick, but included three copies outlined in the Notice of Hearing letter. Mark had been getting himself even more antsy as he'd been texting with Corbin and Rob who had both been through the process and who advised him that it could take all day. He wanted us to notify Alan, our lawyer right away, and I tried to calm him by saying, "Whatever will be, will be. We'll figure it out when we get there." The lawyer was expecting to be there for a couple of hours, regardless. Mark was more afraid of what the lawyer's bill would be. We both took our own vehicles, as we both had to go to work afterwards. Mark didn't want to park downtown, so at first, he suggested that I pick him up at Evan's Lumber, then as he headed out the door at 8:00, he said, never mind, I'll walk from Evan's. My instinct was to be fearful that he wouldn't make it to the 8:30 registration, but I told myself, the walk will calm his nerves and the hearing was between me and Felix, and my Lawyer said he would be there. As I drove there, I was talking to myself… "This is exciting. This is good. We will do fine." Part of me was not convinced. It was a little cool in the morning but had the potential to be a nice day. I brought my water bottle and chose a navy polka dot dress and three-quarter length white raincoat. I didn't look snooty, and I didn't look like I didn't care. But I was chilled to the bone and I couldn't stop shivering.

I parked in the underground parking lot. I was getting familiar with this place, I thought, as I had been here to file the L1 notice with the Landlord and Tenant Board and also was here for my inquiries about the taxes. I made my way to the elevator and to the main floor and asked directions to "Boardroom C". It was 8:20-8:25, and there was a kind, older gentlemen dressed formally in his security or officer attire to have everyone sign in. He said we were the twenty-third on the list but would be bumped up if the tenant did not show as it would be non-contested.

I hoped Felix wouldn't show.

Mark walked in, with his coffee in hand, wearing his brown zip up sweater and jeans. He really had lost weight and his face was weary. I told him to sign in before he sat down. The room was like a large classroom with tables connected end to end facing the front where the judge's table was. There were two tables placed for the opposing parties to plead their cases. It occurred to me that this could be a very long day to have to listen to all of these cases. Alan showed up in his black suit and tie, carrying his briefcase. I was glad he came, thought he walked very slowly and guarded, as he'd had prostate and kidney issues of late. Once he sat between Mark and I, I knew this was the right decision. He made small talk and helped to neutralize some of the static in the air from our nerves. He asked me a few more questions to sort things out then Felix walked in. He had no paperwork on him and he was alone. He avoided eye contact and sat at the back table, diagonally behind us. We were in the third row from the front.

I think we all had a unified mental obscenity, upon seeing him enter. "Shit!" This would be a long day. Alan fidgeted a bit, then mumbled something about mediation and went up to speak to the lawyers. It was announced that anyone that wanted to go and speak with a lawyer could, and that there was also a Mediator available. The lady that took her seat at the judge's table mentioned that cell phone pictures would not be admissible as evidence. Three copies of evidence would be needed as outlined in the Notice of Hearing Letter. I remembered Felix having taken some pictures of insulation that he suspected to have mould.

Alan then went to speak to Felix and came back to say he was willing to go to mediation. After the judge finished her introduction, the mediator called us to join her in an adjacent empty room. This was a little less formal and I allowed Alan to do most of the talking. When asked if he acknowledged not paying rent, Felix mentioned that he was hospitalized for the last three weeks. She directly asked him when he would be moving out. He hummed and hawed and she said to give an exact date. He said, "Next month, I guess." She wrote down June 30, 2016. He tried to bring up issues, but he was shot down by the mediator to say that this is about non-payment of rent. She articulated to him, that if he was still residing at the rental property that a Sheriff would physically remove him from the property, after the agreed upon date. We will have been supporting Felix now for seven months.

We brought up our concern over his unpaid bill being transferred to our taxes as this was a possibility for the water bill, which stays with the house. The Mediator wrote a deadline of June 10 to provide us with copies of the hydro, gas and water bills and that we should be taking a final hydro (water) meter reading on June 30. He regressed when he knew he could say nothing to challenge and we all walked to Boardroom C to make our agreement official. The proceedings were interrupted so that the judge could hear our case.

After repeating the agreement to us, Felix spoke up about some issues with the house and the judge also stopped him to say, this is not about that, this is about you not paying rent and if you have issues to take it up with the Supreme Court.

As we were adjourned, and walked into the Hallway to take our leave, Mark stopped to have us clarify things to Felix, as he seemed confused about the financial part. Alan suggested that it was a sweet deal we were giving him, and Mark said "This is what you wanted." Felix didn't seem so sure. Mark explained that Felix could get what remained of the deposit money held in trust, less the rent owed, and damages incurred to the property on their behalf. Originally, he had planned to 'rent-to-own'. After the move, he would have to visit Alan's office for his check.

Finally, I felt a little relief from the months and years this had been weighing on us.

Mark still seemed uneasy. Once we got to the car, I turned to him and said, "This was good, enjoy it a little. Smile." But he was in a broken record scenario, playing it over to try to find something else to stress out about. Finally, we were able to move forward on this. I just had to convince him to leave it be, and let me continue as planned. He was still so fragile.

I dropped him to his truck at Evan's Lumber, and he was anxious to get going. He suddenly turned on his heel and popped back in the car to give me a kiss and say goodbye. I felt hopeful.

Once at work in the parking lot, I texted Mom, Dad, Mel and my boss Doreen, as I knew they would be waiting for some news.

I got to work by 10:00, and felt pretty proud about how things had gone.

Mark had to go to a meeting that night, and I thought it would be lovely to have a glass of wine to celebrate this achievement. I went downstairs to ask Dad if he had any wine. I asked him to put it in my coffee mug and we both went to sit by the water. He told me how proud he was of me a few times before this, but he also said, "Jan, you are a leader. You have amazing strength, and you know what that lady said to you about losing your power...I think you got it back!"

That was a moment that will stick with me. My Dad was such a wonderful, consistent support beam for this house of mine. I felt so very lucky to have him here.

I realized that the destination in life is not some time in the future, it's from the successful journey within. I was learning something about myself.

CHAPTER NINE

Please, Just Hold the Umbrella for Me?

Things had been going so well. I thought maybe it might be time to lose the dark hair, which I'd worn through these difficult couple of years, my "dark ages". In January, I was even able to sell the house in Dowling, and almost had a bidding war, but the second family couldn't get pre-approval for a mortgage due to the stricter rules for new homeowners that came into effect that fall. I took a cash deal with no conditions, for $15 000 less than the asking price. I was so relieved to not have to shovel that driveway, anymore. It was worth it just to have one less thing to worry about. The other two properties were rented, so getting rid of them wasn't such a priority.

Christmas was quiet, but nice and I verbalized my pride in Mark for doing so well at staying off the alcohol and told him that he looked so much better this Christmas than he did last year. He didn't say much, this type of conversation always made him uncomfortable.

He still spent his evenings and thirteen out of fourteen nights on the couch downstairs, and if I hadn't told him that I was going for a breast biopsy, he would never have known.

Ian and Dad were the only ones that I had physical contact with, most days. I looked forward to their daily hugs. Ian hugged me with his soul at least once a day which was why he suspected something was up during the week of my biopsy. I was more careful with pressure to my chest and didn't join him in the hot tub. I thought the kids really did know us both pretty well and would probably have some fun ideas, for this project that was inspired by a question and answer survey that I saw on social media. I wanted Mark and I to spend more time together, one on one, but wasn't sure how to achieve it. Ian eagerly rose to the challenge of making up date ideas for me and Mark. He was so cute in writing them up on little pieces of paper, which he folded and placed in our new "Mom and Dad's Date Jar". One of which read "Go to the cinema, and share a popcorn if you wish.", another was "Feed the kids early. Eat together later and then have a hot tub." These were simple yet beautiful ideas, and very reasonable.

One night, Ian was searching high and low as Mark had blamed him for losing Mark's high-speed cell phone charger. In his thorough search, Ian went downstairs to check the couch but Mark stopped him and said he'd already checked there. Ian came up to my room, as I was watching 'Westworld' on the Android box, to say he thought Dad was trying to hide something in the couch because he was acting really strange. Ian snuck downstairs again, when Mark was in the kitchen, and found an empty bottle under the couch cushion where Mark usually plants himself. He avoided his father as he immediately brought the bottle up to me to ask if it was booze. It was an empty mickey of vodka. My head bowed at this discovery. We were so disappointed, and Ian apologized and asked me not to tell Dad that he was the one to find it.

I touched base with Mark's co-worker in Espanola to see if she had noticed anything and she said that their co-worker Pam, had noticed that one day he smelled of mouthwash or cologne and that she assumed he was drinking again, because he had been complaining more about his feet.

God give me strength.

I left it out the next day, and asked Mark about it. He said he just wanted to feel normal again, and that he had only bought that at New Year's and it had lasted that long. I reiterated that he could not drink anything. It was a problem.

The Doctor's office called me to go in to discuss my biopsy results. Abby was with me, and saw the Doctor first. When it was my turn, I sent her to the waiting room. Dr. Sawkiw told me that the persistent lump in my right breast was in fact breast cancer. I had Invasive Ductal Carcinoma, and he would refer me to a surgeon. It was a difficult thing to tell Mark, Mom, Dad and the kids, but I felt it was important to keep them informed. I emphasized to the kids, that it could be as easy as having it removed, and not to panic, though my tears may have deceived me during those conversations.

So, it continued. Mark expressed a few times how he wanted to feel 'normal' again. Each time I discouraged drinking and told him it was not normal to hide it. It seemed to take the back burner for a short while as my lumpectomy and sentinel node biopsy took center stage.

Mark came with me to see Dr. Benedict for the results of my lumpectomy and it was so very positive. The tissue around the breast cancer had no cancer (clear margins), and the Doc mentioned that they took out more lymph nodes than expected, a good twenty or so, which were also clear. Wonderful news! I mentioned that I had some discomfort in my rib, and wondered if it was from the way I was healing but it didn't seem to pose a concern to the surgeon, and Mark and I went for lunch at a little Mexican diner at the next corner. I celebrated with a delicious tortilla soup and chicken chimichanga.

It felt surreal. Perhaps, I was prepared for worse news, and knew that I should be happy and celebrate being cancer free, but those feelings weren't flowing readily. I shared my happy news with my work family and continued to work full time.

My one rib almost felt like it had a pinched nerve, so I went to see my Chiropractor. I was in such pain and sobbed when she tried to manipulate me, so she taped me instead. I felt like such a baby! She figured I had a couple of slipped ribs. Mark recommended that I try acupuncture to relieve my increasing pain. I was getting palpitations daily and wondered if my thyroid levels were off again. But, from the first acupuncture appointment, the palpitations subsided and I attributed them to anxiety. I had to stop walking Charlie in the morning because he pulled the leash and would really yank it if he encountered any other animals on our walks.

One morning, he pulled with such a sudden jolt, that it caused me a great deal of pain. It almost took my breath away. It took everything for me to get home. As soon as I walked in the door, I was bent in two and in tears. When Mark saw the state I was in, he dropped onto the orange oversized ottoman of the entrance chair and cried with me. He said I was not to walk the dog anymore. It pained me to see him hurt for me, but also gave me a flutter of warmth with the thought that he still loved me.

I stayed home with my pain one day as it took everything to get out of bed and thought I had better see a Medical Doctor about this. My Doctor's office was closed, it was a Thursday, so, I went to their associate clinic in Minnow Lake. I painfully drove myself there and slowly walked in to grab a number and register. It didn't take too long to get in and I had a female Doctor that poked and prodded and advised that I go to the hospital to have a chest X-ray done. So, I drove to the hospital and was in and out so fast, I didn't get charged for parking.

Back at work for 8:30 Monday morning, and I got a call first thing by Simone at my Doctor's office. She wanted me to come in right away to discuss my pain. At first, I was worried but once I got there, she asked me where I had gone for my X-ray. This gave me some relief that the results weren't necessarily bad, as they didn't even have the results yet.

Once in to see Dr. Sawkiw, he said that the chest X-ray showed some fluff in my right shoulder and above my lumpectomy of my right breast. He said I think we'll send you for a Bone-scan to make sure it's not a metastasis from the breast cancer. It felt like I was punched in the chest. "Pardon me?" I was no longer prepared for this kind of news. The margins and lymph nodes were clear! Maybe it was from another, undiagnosed tumour? The following Wednesday, was my first appointments with both medical and radiology Oncologists. They decided to wait for my scan and added a Cat-scan to the Bone-scan for that Friday, before they decided how we would proceed on treatment. The following Monday, the Oncology nurse called my cell phone and asked me to come and see both Oncologists for 11:30 that morning. It was my day off as I worked on Saturday, and was at Mom's for breakfast. Mom asked if I'd like her to come with me and I thought that might be a good idea, in case the news was bad. Dr. Noble was the first to see me and was quite blunt, which I did respect, but still found startling. He said: "Your breast cancer has spread. You have metastases in multiple ribs, vertebrae and small nodules on the surface of your lungs and an enlarged lymph node in the lung. Now, we have to treat you as palliative."

'**Palliative**'. A very scary word, which both Mom and I associated with 'imminent death'.

The nurse, Megan, tried to reassure me that 'palliative' just means that it is not curable, and we would treat to manage my pain, and that I could live many years, yet.

All I could think about was what this would do to Mark and the kids, and I wept.

We went for a very late lunch, and as Mom tried to comfort me, I also tried to comfort her. We were both in shock. When I got home, Abby was just heading for a nap and Ian was busy and Mark was still on his way home from work.

I went downstairs to tell Dad. He gave me support and a hug and promised he'd help with anything and that we would get through this.

After composing myself a bit, Mark came downstairs looking for me. Dad and I were still sitting together on the couch in Dad's apartment. Mark said "how did it go?", as he knew I had been called in to see the Oncologists. Dad's voice grew shaky and emotional, as he said "you have to tell him, Jan".

I started to cry, and Mark fell sideways, into a quasi-fetal position, onto the nearest chair and sobbed "NO...NO...NO...NO...no... noooo...!". I slowly got up, as changes in position hurt, and I tried to be as clear as I could to give him the facts and rubbed his back. Again, I felt loved, but also felt a little robbed by him not offering me a hug or support. The kids had been aware of the initial breast cancer diagnosis and I wasn't going to keep this from them. Looking back to when my ribs first started to give me grief, Ian asked me if it was from the cancer, which I was certain it was not, at the time. It was hard not to cry when telling them my news but they took it very well, at first. It took some time to process and resulted in the need for a few missed school days. Ian was having difficulty sleeping and concentrating at school. Abby found concentration a bit of a challenge.

After a couple more weeks, the Radiology Oncologist planned to try to alleviate my most acute pain in my lower right back with five consecutive days of intensive radiation treatment. I had a burst-fracture only millimeters away from my spine. My breasts were no longer the concern. The radiation procedure was as easy as an X-ray, but getting off of the hard table was excruciating. Once started, I had inflammation that made my back hurt not only when I changed positions, but all of the time. I stayed home from work since being told of the metastases and tried different pain meds. I was given Tramacet, Oxycocet, and Hydromorphone. None of them took the edge off of the pain, but they all made me severely constipated, despite the stool softeners, pills to take "in case of constipation", the hot drinks, and prunes. I was so constipated, that when straining on the toilet, I heard and felt a rib "pop" on the left side, the "good" side.

I stopped the pain meds. Instead the Radiology Oncologist recommended aggressive ibuprofen therapy, to see if an anti-inflammatory would help. At least my bowel returned to normal function but now with a dislocated rib on my good side, getting up from lying down, especially off the radiation table was sheer agony.

My radiation week was my most painful and that's when I noticed the warning signs in Mark's demeanor that he was spiraling downhill and drinking again. His breath reeked. He wore the same clothes for multiple days, and his demeanor was telltale. On the Wednesday of this most painful week, I tried to muster as much strength as I could to talk to him. I was mad too, because the kids needed supper and I was unable to lift a pan into the stove or do any meal preparation. He wasn't cooking, or he was coming home late. Mark listened to me without denying that he has been drinking. I said my peace then went upstairs. Abby went down to give him a piece of her mind and proceeded to check his vehicle for alcohol. She found a water bottle with rye in it under his front seat. Later he came up to our room where I was watching the television, and he paced. I bit my lip as I tried to ignore that he kept walking into the bloom of my hibiscus and would knock it off, if he continued. He started to talk, after some time. He brought up all kinds of things, mostly the same things he would usually bring up in his "woe is me state", that I thought I had addressed these same issues time and time again…

1. How many times have we had sex in the last couple of years? *(If you'd come to bed every night, and maybe look at me or talk to me during the day, I may be more inclined. I'm not attracted to you when you've been drinking, and I'm bitter when you only come to bed because you expect sex. Not happening!)*
2. Why do you have a password on your phone?

(Most people do. It helps to avoid pocket dialing. I do my banking on my phone, and don't want to be more at risk)

3. I'm trying to figure out if you are like your Mom, she always had secrets from your Dad.
   (Ok, this was a new one. What are you talking about? I have no secrets.)

4. Why don't you let me read your diary?
   (Diaries are personal and private. Yes, I'm writing an autobiography based on my diaries, and one day when I'm ready, I may share it.)

5. We used to be happy
   (When you are drinking, only you think you are happy. I'm happy when you spend time with me. The kids make me happy. Our friends and neighbours make me happy. I told him he needs to find a new definition for "happiness".)

6. We don't go on trips anymore because of you
   (Not the past two years, as I didn't want to an all-inclusive and make staying sober that much more difficult)

7. We used to have company
   (You were always the one to invite people over or make plans. The neighbours are very supportive, and understand that you are no longer drinking, and all you have to do is call them!)

8. He asked me if I still want him around as I told him before that I wasn't going through this again.
   (Alcoholism is a disease. You are my family, I want to be with you. And, I am in no shape to be doing any packing.)

How could I leave him, even if I wanted to? I couldn't even pack a bag. I told him it feels like he was trying to push me away by doing this, but I told him that I needed him healthy to take care of me and the kids right now.

Ian had been eavesdropping. When Mark left the bedroom, I went to the bathroom and sobbed. Ian came upstairs and hugged me admitting that he had heard everything. He was devastated and was convinced that we were breaking up. He was so distressed, that he went to cry with his Grandpa. Dad came up shaking and mad that Ian had to feel this way and he verbally expressed his disappointment with Mark. Later, Mark went to talk to Dad alone, but Dad wouldn't let him off the hook with any of his reasons.

Mark promised me he would go back to AA, and would fix this. He went to talk to the social worker at the Cancer Centre on Friday. On Thursday, though, he wasn't home until 8:00 that night and showed up with Corbin. Corbin had also talked to him on behalf of work. I didn't know that they had noticed anything, but it was obvious to us. They had to have noticed it too.

I hoped he would finally get it.

Friday, Mark drove me to my appointment with the Radiology Oncologist, and my last radiation appointment for now. Dr. Bowen answered all of my questions and gave me hope that the Tamoxifen would shrink my metastasis and my pain will be significantly reduced but that these are slow acting. She prescribed me a muscle relaxant for bedtime and a steroid for the day.

Friday was exhausting and I finally slept an entire night. Saturday was sunny and beautiful. Dad brought my lawn chair and ottoman on the patio, and Mark put the cushions on it and I was able to sit and read almost pain free. It was a lovely and much needed break. I had a few neighbours visit and that week we had food donations of spaghetti sauce, chicken meatballs, a turkey pot pie casserole, lasagna, chocolate quinoa cake, homemade cream puffs and cookies. I felt so blessed.

The couple of days following that most terrible week. I gradually had a noticeable reduction to my pain. Position changes remained the most difficult but I was starting to believe that in a few weeks, I would be more mobile and maybe back to work. The Social Media "Living Metastatic One Day at a Time" and "Closed Metastatic" were Stage IV support groups that I joined had women living 2-3-4-7-12-15, up to 20 years with metastatic breast cancer. This was reassuring that my demise wasn't as impending, as we first thought.

I made social work appointments for both Abby and Ian, but Ian was so private that after the first session, he did not want to go back, complaining that the social worker had bad coffee breath. Abby optimized her session and booked eight more. Mark became more doting since our talk, and his visit with the social worker. He was always asking if I needed help and actually volunteered the words, that I so rarely heard "I love you", as he held my hand in bed.

I was really moved by the support I had been receiving by family, friends and neighbours both near and far. At first, I wasn't sure if posting my cancer progression to social media was going to be well received but I appreciated the well wishes and the love I have felt as a result. It strengthened me. It also saved Mark and the kids having to repeatedly share the difficult news. Now, that I was feeling much less pain, and more mobility, I felt more hopeful that I could still live with some quality for a few years. I've found some stats on the internet that women with Breast Cancer metastases average a survival time of three years, with only 20% making it to five years. I hoped that with being hormone positive (ER+, PR+, HER2neu-), my young age and positive attitude, I would be a good candidate to be a long term METAvivor. I read that if it's only spread to the bones, the prognosis is better, but I also had nodules on my lungs.

Three weeks after the radiation therapy, the pain had significantly reduced, though I still had limitations. I almost felt like the old me. This had been good for Mark and the kids to witness, to confirm that I was not checking out soon. Mark only went for one more social work appointment, then he said that his Social Worker told him she was "done with him". I wished Mark had fulfilled his promise about going back to Alcoholics Anonymous meetings, but he didn't seem to remember making that promise.

After many years, his eldest sister, Mary, came to visit with her husband, Romeo. Mary had moved from Sault Ste Marie to Chatham for a position with H & R Block years ago, and since Romeo wasn't close enough to take his pension from Algoma Steel, he had stayed with the kids for a few more years in the Sault until he could retire. When Romeo retired, Mary was living in Windsor and they sold the house in Sault Ste Marie, and Romeo joined her there. I don't know how they managed living apart for so many years.

We had a nice visit and Mary did all of the cooking and dishes and even made one of my favourites, her strawberry-rhubarb pie. She made four of them and one apple from Dad's leftover apples. She froze them all for us to enjoy later. May was always a busy month. This year Abby turned sixteen on the 10th, I turned forty-five on the 12th, Mom turned seventy on the 13th and Mary turned sixty-three on the 14th. Mel and Mason's wedding Anniversary was May 15th.

I was so spoiled that week. Mark had been going for walks with me in the evenings, I loved that. I was very slow and they were very short, but they were quality time for me. Sometimes he would take Charlie, and sometimes Abby would join us. To celebrate my birthday, which fell on a Friday, our neighbours Colette and Bob, made us dinner and made a chocolate cake that Colette had Abby decorated, right after school. Colette had invited a few neighbours and book buddies to pop in to give me their well wishes. It was a lovely get together, and I thought Mark would have enjoyed it. Instead, he moped around and was miserable. Five people asked me what was wrong with him. I took it as him looking for sympathy. It was embarrassing to have to make excuses for him again.

When we got home, Mark was still in a very sour mood. He didn't talk about it and I really didn't want to open that discussion for another self-pity party or 'when did we have sex last' discussion. It was my birthday and I needed a break from the drama. I felt a little selfish, but I thought I finally had the right to be. I told the kids that addictions are difficult to get over, and he was bound to have some rough days. I felt somewhat responsible though, as a couple of days prior, I brought up that while we were feeling good, we should plan our funerals and update our wills. He wasn't too keen on the idea of funeral arranging but I said to him that many women with metastatic breast cancer survive an average of three years. That could be a reality that he was trying to process that day. My bad. I just want him to be prepared, and if he became a zombie again when my time is up, he wouldn't be a very good decision maker. I wanted to have everything arranged, including Power of Attorney for my personal care.

I also suggested that when this hormone therapy stopped working, that I would have a hard time getting out of bed again like when I was at my worst, so we should start shopping for an adjustable bed. That would also give me peace of mind for my next relapse. I was just trying to be realistic.

Dad was very sensitive, and noted Mark's bad days and felt it was his fault. One day, Dad and I were standing on the back patio by the garage, when he asked me if I wanted him to move out. Argh! No! I told him that me and the kids needed him here. Besides, who would take care of the yard and house maintenance issues? It was frustrating to me that I had to support everyone else emotionally. Restoration of my strength came from meditation and small gestures and tokens from my network of friends and family. I made myself a 'Strong Box', in which I kept these tokens, next to my bed.

I received a parcel in the mail from my childhood friend, Kristi, who had had her own family and moved to New Zealand. She sent a card, a handwritten letter and some very thoughtful gifts. One of which was from her daughter, Sabina, who was inspired by her childhood stories of when Kristi and I were young. Sabina looked very much like Kristi as a child, and had inherited Kristi's Smurf collection that we would have played with and she sent one of the originals to me, the "First Aid Smurf". She made my day. Her words were so kind, that they erased any residual resentment that young me had when she stopped being my best friend in Grade Six. My heart was broken at the time, but I grew from that experience.

Sometimes, we have to hurt, because the healing makes us who we become. Another thoughtful gift from Kristi was the "Pounamu" or greenstone pendant, a symbol in the Maori culture which is given as a gift to someone who's "mana" you respect and wish to honour. She described "mana" as the recognized respect, wisdom, strength and authority of someone who's earned it. I like to think her words are true and that I have a powerful "mana". I will keep these, and the other gifts, I have received with me to remind me of this, and of the love everyone has shown me. These things all gave me a much-needed boost.

My days off work seemed to get so busy. I'd rest, work on my book, go for walks, and once I was able to drive again, I would go to town once in a while for shopping, appointments or lunch dates. Staying still for too long or too much activity would hurt, so I tried to keep a balance. I was able to get a pedicure, then a haircut and some blonde streaks into my hair with my favourite hairdresser, Michelle at Hair Expressions in Garson. That was very heartening. I gave up on any ambition to get reconstruction, and named my now, nipple-less right breast, "Benny, the Angry Blowfish". The horizontal scar spanned most of the breast, looking like a bit of a frown, thus the name. I tried to find humour in the little things.

I spent two and a half hours on a lunch date with my retired co-workers: Doreen and Fran. When I told them that I was aiming to return to work, half days by June, they both thought I was crazy. For everything that I had been through, emotionally and physically, they encouraged me to take the time, and not rush going back. They gave me food for thought. Inside, I was so conflicted. I was so anxious to get back to some normalcy, yet if I only had three years to live, did I want to spend it working? I decided to give myself a few more weeks to see how I felt.

It was time to heal.

A couple of days later, during one of her visits to do my laundry for me, Mom told me that she would be going for surgery on Ian's birthday, June 1st. At first, she thought the lump was at the base of her breast, near her ribs, but the lump was actually in the pleura of her right lung. It had appeared in the fall after her Baltic Cruise in 2015, when she returned with pneumonia, then had increased in size thereby causing concern. They wouldn't know how big a surgery it would be until they operated, but they hoped to remove it with the scopes. Mom didn't want to tell me her news, but I found it easy to remain strong for her, as we didn't know anything about it yet.

I told her she could stay with us for a while if she needed help in the beginning. I could feed her at least, and keep an eye on her. If she needed physical help, maybe Dad, Mark or the kids could help her.

I'd been doing much research about alternative therapies for cancer, and it was adding to my hope, that maybe a combined therapy might just nuke it. I continued to take the Tamoxifen, but I also meditated every day, drank Essiac, Matcha and Chaga teas and ate apricot kernels. I diluted Frankincense, Myrrh and Sandalwood essential oils in Grapeseed oil and put them on a roller ball to rub onto my back along all of my affected bones. I bought an electric, wrap around, heating pad to increase the temperature near to my bone metastases, in hopes that they are less resilient than the healthy cells to the added heat. Each day that Mark rubbed the oils on me, I felt more pain, like when I was having inflammation from the radiation. In my mind, I imagined that the oils were working at killing the tumours, and that's why it was tender. My focus became getting healthy, exercising and trying to boost my immune system. Maybe I could defy the odds or conquer it altogether. I needed to be around, and I was determined to make it happen.

One night, Ian talked to me about Mark as he felt like he was being too secretive again. He suspected he was drinking. I wondered if that was the real reason that Mark stopped taking the pre-gabalin for his neuropathy a week prior. I thanked Ian but assured him that he didn't have to play detective.

The next morning, was a holiday Monday, and after Mark asked me how I was doing, I followed up with "How are you doing? How are the cravings? Are you finding it difficult?" To which he replied "I had a couple of beers when I went out with the curling team last week. I just want to feel normal. Trust me." I asked him if that was why he quit taking the neuropathy meds and he explained that they weren't helping anyway. I stewed all day. I knew him. I knew how he felt, but this felt like a slap in the face. He chose alcohol over me. I didn't want to react right away, I needed time.

Finally, as we were preparing supper, he suggested we go on a weekend away to Toronto. He saw my face as I was fighting with my emotions, and asked me what was going on. I said I'm really uncomfortable with you drinking at all. It makes me nervous and it makes the kids nervous. He didn't say much and quickly changed the subject and was as pleasant as possible. I felt worn out. I had nothing left to fight him with on this.

TEN

Compromise?

One day Mark came home from work, feisty. It started with a disagreement between us about paying for the local ad newspaper, the 'Northern Life', because in his opinion they received enough money from the advertisements. I felt that $3 was not going to break the bank, and we could afford it. Besides, I would be embarrassed to refuse to pay. This intensified his mood and he took issue on the littlest of things. After supper, I asked him to take me for a walk. He agreed to join me, and so did Abby. When he realized Abby was coming, he tried to retract his offer, saying he'd been on his legs all day. I told him that I wanted him to join us. His mood needed it.

His shoulders dropped in losing this battle, and he scowled as he got ready. As we walked, Abby and Charlie were ahead of us, and Mark was next to me and I snuck my hand into his. He made a couple more negative comments. My cell phone went off in my back pocket when Dad texted me, in the voice of Fozzie Bear from the Muppet Show: "You have a text from your Father. Waka-Waka!".

Mark then complained that I never reply when 'he' texts me. I was getting thin on patience. I told him that "I get the same notification when you text me. I am not always immediately able to reply, and sometimes my ringer is off. What is going on with you, today? Why are you so grumpy?". Finally, when we didn't take the closer street "Montcalm", as I wanted to walk to the next street for my new circuit "Puska-Brunet-Aldège", he started to complain again about his legs. I let go of his hand, and raised my voice "Just go home, we will walk the rest of the way!". I was pissed off and made it known. In response, he sped up so that he was walking ten feet ahead of me. We walked in a line with many feet apart, Abby and Charlie were between us now. When Abby waited for me, Mark was forty feet ahead and not looking back, but he was still taking the same route as us, on the opposite side of the road. I was no match for Mark's ego.

I had come to the conclusion that when given the choice between me and alcohol, I was certain that alcohol was Mark's soul-mate. I thought about my experiences with the support group for families touched by alcohol addiction, and how these Al-Anon meetings hadn't met my needs. They had given the two options of leaving the alcoholic or letting things be in God's hands. I chose to take the bull by the horns and make a third option, one of change. But so far, that had not been an easy journey.

The fence-sitter in me, started to wonder about the Alcoholics Anonymous meetings that Mark had attended and why he didn't want to go back. Could it be that they were not offering him reasonable options, either? Before he was prescribed this neuropathy medicine, pre-gabalin, he was a heavy, daily drinker but usually this did not make him a Zombie. Perhaps, that the solution was in this third option. That of change and reform, perhaps in a compromise?

I wondered if he continued to stay off of this medication, would he be able to drink, with control? Could I trust him to learn to drink responsibly with some agreed upon limitations? It would have to be a written behavioral contract, as perhaps then he would be made accountable and could easily review the conditions when he needed reminding. I did not want to be the reason for him going off the deep end, but I did not want him to remain so unhappy and angry with me. I also needed him to be there for me as my husband again and caregiver when I needed it. I needed to find an incentive that was more enticing to him than keeping us together.

I considered the following stipulations:

1. *If I have to take pre-gabalin or other medications for neuropathy where alcohol is contraindicated, I must abstain from all alcohol consumption.*
2. *I will not drink alone.*
3. *I will not go alone to a restaurant or bar, and drink with the patrons there, unless the rendez-vous was pre-arranged.*
4. *I will not keep alcohol in the house.*
5. *When going to social functions, I will have two drinks maximum per day, not more than twice per week, i.e. One drink = beer <20 oz, 1 oz liquor or spirits with mix, 6 oz glass of wine.*
6. *If I am at a function or activity with the kids, before having alcohol, I will ask the children if they would be comfortable getting a ride with me, if I have a drink. I will not pressure them. I will respect their decision, as I am their caregiver. This applies to all motorized vehicles, for road or water. I will not put my children in danger for my selfishness.*
7. *I will not drink because it was a stressful day.*
8. *If we have company, and they bring their own booze, that booze will go back with them.*
9. *I will not drive if those two drinks were consumed within the hour.*
10. *I realize that my family has been repeatedly, emotionally hurt by my drinking, and they are uncomfortable with me having alcohol again. I will use this opportunity to prove to them that I can be trusted again, but I will not go back to drinking.*
11. *If I fail at the above, I will not hesitate to start back at Alcoholic Anonymous meetings, and go back to the Detox clinic, if I am requested to do so.*

I contemplated adding consequences to this contract, based on his being accountable and holding to the terms, but how truthful would he be, if the consequences may lead to him having to move out? The social worker once asked me what my limits were. Honestly, I really was afraid to set them. Was I the only one wanting to stay married? If we were better communicators, I wouldn't have had the need to consider such a formality. It felt so cold, and I hated it.

Agreement between Mark and Jan- draft

I, Mark...commit to remain truthful and abide by the above drinking limitations set by my wife and kids with our best interests in mind. These are very generous allowances for someone with my drinking history. I understand, that this compromise is only because Jan loves me and wishes to stand by me and suspects that my worst states have been a result of a combination of alcohol and the neuropathy medication. Of my own accord, I have chosen to stop taking the pregabalin, as it was not helping alleviate the discomfort in my feet, and this was not forced upon me. Jan is only making this contract because of the accentuated effects that small amounts of alcohol have on me when I take this medication, and that she thinks I would choose alcohol over her. I will try not to be selfish, and realize that my problems affect my family, too. Prior to taking this medication, I had a drinking problem, and I must not go back to this daily drinking pattern, despite what habits my friends may have. Failure to meet the above expectations may result in my being requested to find an apartment, or other living arrangements, loss of a business partner or valued employees, loss of driver's license and disappointment in me by my wife, children and peers. Any emotional or psychological stresses that are too much for me to handle, I will follow up with a social worker, support group or equivalent. I realize that despite their love for me, my family cannot endure anymore relapses on my behalf.

I, Jan...commit to this marriage in my support to make Mark better, provided that he keeps himself in line with this contract. I love him, I want him as my husband. I want to grow old with him. I want to know that I can depend on him when my health should turn again. I hope that he will do this for us and for the kids. For our happiness.

I sat on this contract for a while. It terrified me. How would he respond to this? I hoped that he'd see it as it was intended. A solution for both of us, so that we could move forward.

But then, camp happened. He went for a second weekend to bring up the second boat. He was supposed to go fishing with Kari, but called me later Saturday afternoon to say he had vomited on the boat and that he still was feeling unwell. I told him to have a Gatorade and rest. He said he would be home early on Sunday.

Sunday morning it rained off and on, for most of the day, and I thought I'd better get the spaghetti sauce ingredients prepared. We usually made this recipe together. Mark would brown the hamburger and adjust the spices, and I would puree all of the coarse vegetables so that the kids wouldn't see them and still eat their veggies. We usually made enough to fill two large roast pans would cook them at 300°F for 3 hours. We would have a nice batch to freeze in plastic freezer bags for quick dinners.

That afternoon Mom and I had our book club gathering so I left the roast pans filled with sauce in the oven, and told Abby that they were there. Mark still wasn't home at 1:15, when we left for book club. But I figured they'd be okay on low while I was gone.

We had a lovely afternoon with the Lakeside Book Buddies, and we had a delicious feast. We all usually bring some munchies. It was late afternoon when we adjourned. We usually finish around 4:00, but we didn't get home until 5:00. Mark still hadn't returned home.

And the spaghetti sauce was starting to get a little dark on top. I got Abby to lift them out of the oven for me, and started making her wheat free noodles, first. We'd been trying to figure out if the pain in her belly was from a wheat sensitivity or not, so she'd been staying off of wheat for a few weeks.

I called Mark to find he was driving home, and would be home by 6:00.

By 6:00, he had arrived. He had a quick shower, adorned some cologne, and was oddly upbeat at dinner.

Abby's demeanor was off. I asked her what was going on, but she didn't elaborate.

I tried spending some time with Mark, downstairs after supper, but decided to head upstairs to watch a show. He turned the downstairs television off and said he'd join me in our room.

On our way, I made sure Ian was getting ready for bed, it was 9:10. But, I couldn't find Abby. I even went to Dad's apartment, but instead of finding Abby, I found Mom and Dad talking. They hadn't seen Abby in a while, so I assumed she was watching TV in our loft bedroom. Finally, I found her sitting in the dark, front entrance. She was crying. I sat with her to ask what was making her so sad. She explained that she hadn't wanted to tell me all evening that she found more booze in her Dad's car and had confronted him. "I just want him to stop!" She sobbed but she was angry. Mark came in and she snapped at him "I'm not talking to you!", and she stormed away. Mark looked at me, as he lowered himself onto the wooden bench facing me on the ottoman of the big orange chair in our front entrance. I remained calm, and not too emotional. I repeated several times that we needed him to start taking care of himself. He needed to make an appointment with his family physician and ask for a referral to a neurologist. He had to start going to Alcoholics Anonymous meetings again.

His responses kept me convinced that he was still in denial about alcohol being a problem. He still blamed me, for making this an issue. He said that he would be there for me and the kids but I asked him what that really meant. I explained that I loved him and wanted to grow old with him. I also explained that stress is not good for my longevity and that these up and downs are killing me. It needed to stop and he needed to stop drinking. I also told him that he should talk to Abby before bed, to apologize and say that he would work at this. Otherwise, I didn't think that she could sleep through the night.

Abby was hiding in Ian's closet and he was playing with his cell phone on his bed. Mark came in but said he was going downstairs, and started for the family room. He came back to signal that we were supposed to join him as he didn't want to talk with my Mom in ear shot in the next room. She was staying in Abby's room for a few days to recover from her lumpectomy.

We followed him like little ducklings, in a line all the way to the basement. Immediately, he got comfy on the couch and turned the TV on. Ian crawled in behind me perpendicular to Mark on the brown comfy sectional couch and Abby faced us all, but remained standing with her arms crossed. We waited expectantly for him to speak. Abby had a very confrontational look about her. She asked him to shut off the TV if he wanted to talk. He did so, but sat tongue-tied for a very long time. Finally, he said, "We've been going through a lot lately" ... That's really all he said. I tried to encourage him to say what we wanted to hear, by summarizing what I had asked of him. When he didn't contribute much more, Abby left. I tried to get Ian ready for bed, and he was frustrated. "This keeps happening!", he protested. I was running out of excuses and ways to comfort them. Abby cried some more and told me that it's her fault when things go wrong, that whenever she spoke up, it ended badly. I told her that she didn't need to police her father, and that being open and honest was a good thing. I told her that I didn't catch on this time, but it was definitely not her fault that he had been drinking. She hinted that she didn't want to go to school the next day after this. I told her she had been missing too much school. I had a feeling though, that neither of them would sleep again that night.

Mark didn't stay in our bed all night and finished his morning sleep on the downstairs couch. When I came out of my room, I found both kids sitting in the living room looking at me, expectantly. Neither of them looked rested, and I told them they could stay home. I also told them that when their Dad comes up to get ready, I would give him the choice to go to AA or move out. Ian seemed to understand better this time that I wanted this marriage to work but had to perform a little tough love to knock some sense into his Dad.

Mark came upstairs and got ready and approached me for a hug. I returned the embrace and asked him If he remembered our conversation from the night before. He nodded and whispered an emotional "Yep". I looked him in the eye and said, "Listen. I love you. I want this to work, but if you don't make the appointment with your Doctor for a referral and start going to Alcoholics Anonymous meetings, you will have to move out. I'm sorry, it has come to this. But, the kids have to stay home again because of this." He seemed shocked by this ultimatum, but didn't say anything. He paced for a bit. He picked up a jacket and started to fold it. I wondered if he was packing a bag. I decided to give him some space and came downstairs to the kitchen. Mom and Abby were sitting on the couch in the living room, reading. Mom reading Abby's e-reader, and Abby was reading on her cell phone. It was eerily quiet.

He didn't say a word then left. He came back a couple of minutes later looking for the dog, as he usually brought Charlie with him to work. Then he left again.

I knew in my heart, that I did the right thing. The choice was now his. I prayed he made the right one.

I alerted Corbin that it may be a rough day, but I didn't reach out to his staff in Espanola.

Abby had already had a coffee to keep her awake for the day. Ian was able to go back to bed, and Mom said she'd stay with them until I got back from my appointment with the social worker. At my social work appointment, I shared the recent events and the ultimatum that I had given Mark. The Social worker remarked that a couple of years ago, I was more mothering to him, and wanted to help him. My limits had since been determined. The burden on my children brought out my Momma bear role. I told her, it was easier for me to be strong for others. Abby texted me to request an iced coffee, and after such a crazy night, I thought I would treat them. I picked a hot chocolate up for Ian as well. Once I got home, I realized that more caffeine probably wasn't the best idea. Abby wouldn't be able to sleep until later in the afternoon, as this was now her second caffeinated product that day. I was relieved that they both managed to get some rest. I picked up some hamburger buns for supper and while I was cooking on the barbecue, Mark arrived home unnoticed and slipped downstairs. Ian had checked on him, as he was supposed to have brought Ian's new cell phone home that day. Mark said he had forgotten it, and was tired. He didn't join us for dinner. After I cleaned up the supper dishes, I received a text message from Mark's co-worker Lisa.

Lisa> "Did he make it home?"

Me> "Yes. And straight to the couch. I was going to text you to see how today went. What happened on your end?

Lisa> "Not good. He was a mess."

Lisa> "I didn't know what to do and when I was gonna pull his keys outta his truck he disappeared."

Me> "Did it seem like he was drinking today? The dog smells of cigarettes."

Me> "This morning, I gave him the choice to go to AA or move out...this stress is killing me...literally!"

Lisa> "Well I was told by three customers that he was hammered. I agree."

Lisa> "I hear ya, not that it is as bad for me, but I'm about ready for a new job if this keeps up, I tell ya! I love my job, but it's a virus. I can't handle the stress either. Feels like babysitting."

Me> "I'm sorry that you have to put up with this all day."

Lisa> "He is not handling the stress well at all. He needs to be supportive, not missing in action."

Me> "I agree. Hard thing to teach. I can't count on him anymore."

Lisa> "No one can. I'm hoping he doesn't show up tomorrow. I don't know how to deal with it and I'm gonna snap on him and he is gonna hate me but he is making himself and all of us look bad."

My nerves were ablaze. It felt like another slap in the face. I wondered if he drank the day of my ultimatum because of stress, or spite. I went down to talk to him, but he was asleep. As I left the basement, I slammed the door. I was furious.

I went for a walk with Abby, before the rain started, but I felt so tense. This was not good for my healing, I thought. I needed to meditate when I got back home. Finally, the next time I went downstairs to see Mark, he was awake, but still lying down on the couch. All I said was "So, I guess you've made your choice?". He was confused, and looked at me for clarification. I said "Three customers thought that you were hammered today!". He was livid. "I did not drink today! Which customers? Who told you that?". I felt cornered, and told him that I didn't know specifically which customers but that Lisa and reached out to me to find out if he had made it home safely, as he seemed to be inebriated. I also mentioned that this news was not surprising to me as he had snuck downstairs upon arriving home, like he used to when he was drinking. I mentioned that he had about a dozen little bottles of vodka in a cooler in the back of his locked truck. He just shook his head with an expression of pain, and he sat up with his elbows resting on his thighs with hands clasped, and started to slap his feet one at a time on the laminate floor. He did this steady while he sat there and stewed. He looked hilarious. He was so dramatic sometimes that he reminded me of a cartoon character. I watched the news, very distractedly, but some things were hard to hear for the repeated foot beating. I said, "Well, I'm glad you weren't drinking, as I would have asked you to slap me. It would hurt less." After a little while longer, with the continued noise of his feet, and his verbal silence, I moved to go upstairs. He was right behind me, and stopped in the kitchen for something to eat. I didn't see any more of him that night, or the next morning.

I slept all night. His side of the bed was still made up from the day before. I got up early, as Ian had to be at his school to catch a bus at 7:45, to be brought to the school soccer tournament in the valley. Mark had originally offered to bring him, but he wasn't up at 7:00, when I got Ian to get out of bed. The only communication we had was when he called me as I was driving back from Chelmsford to tell me that I had left the dog outside. Oops!

The day was busy enough, as I picked up Mom to go to get her stitches out. Her surgery had been a much simpler one, and the lump was well encased, and likely benign. The nurse had told her that she could go to the Ambulatory Care Unit (ACU), to have this done. The nurse was mistaken. We left and went to the YMCA, as I wanted to get a membership and start some water exercise classes to strengthen my back, and she wanted to check into the Pulmonary office there, to see if she needed to sign up for classes. It was very productive. We then picked up coffees at Tim Horton's, when Abby texted that she wanted me to pick her up. "Tough day. Having a hard time focusing and getting things done. I don't think I can make it the rest of the day.". I dropped Mom at the clinic across from where she lives to get her stitches out there, and went back to the other end of town to get Abby. She convinced me to order personal pizzas and we picked them up on our way home.

I didn't hear from Mark, other than an "Okay" to acknowledge that I had brought Abby home. I wondered if he was going to start his AA meetings, or would I have to give him a deadline. I thought I would give it until the end of this week, and then set a deadline one week from then. I hoped I would not have to enforce this, should the time come.

He didn't get home until 7:00 p.m., and he walked slowly and when responding to questions, he only whispered. Ian thought he was drunk. I couldn't tell. Maybe he was just depressed and dramatic. He hardly ate any supper, and laid down on the upstairs couch. I went for a walk. I kept thinking, whether he is drinking or not is not my issue. My request was for him to attend AA meetings.

The fourth night of no meetings, I was short with Mark. He sensed it, and he asked why I was so snippy. I looked at him without wavering and said ... "I'm snippy because this is the fourth day since our talk, and you still haven't gone to AA." He lost his appetite for supper and found the couch on the porch to lay down on. During my walk, he migrated to his regular couch in the basement.

The fifth night, we had lots of leftovers and we ate early. Abby asked me to go for a walk, and while we were out, Mark had arrived home and went downstairs to the couch. He didn't come up all evening or all night. He had texted earlier that day about us going to a Blues festival the next day, which was Saturday. I really felt like he was trying to distract me from my stance. That and a few other comments he made that week: "I started wearing my orthotics again, and my feet haven't been hurting for a week and a half" (though he had been rubbing them together in bed the night before.). He also asked me "Do you find the days long? Would you like to come to work with me one day?". I thanked him but declined as I felt my days were pretty full at home during my sick leave. It felt like he was trying to prove that he could manage without AA, yet every night, the kids thought he had been drinking.

ELEVEN

Tough Love

When describing my character, I often said I was a fence sitter. I went with the flow. I could see both sides to every story and when someone had an issue, I tried to see it from the other perspective. I could justify many things this way, but I felt that I was not a very efficient decision maker because of it. I thought that if I could deny my own needs for that of others', it meant there could be peace. There was happiness to be had when others were happy.

That is, until I finally realized that all of these sacrifices cultured resentment for the neglect of my needs. I was and am just as important as everyone else. Becoming a patient was very humbling, but also enlightening. When the anti-estrogen therapy started shrinking my metastases and pain, I knew I needed to be selfish, and work on boosting my health and minimizing the stress and anything that would be a detriment to my longevity.

I knew that having given Mark the ultimatum to go to AA or move out, was the right move for my health, his health and the mental and physical welfare of our children.

What did he decide?

Mark had been hiding in the basement for most of the week. Saturday was a beautiful, June day. I enjoyed most of the day outside. When I went downstairs and asked him if he wanted some supper. He said he would come upstairs for something to eat. I put away the clean dishes from the dishwasher while he picked at his lasagna. The phone rang and Abby took the portable out of earshot. I took the opportunity to ask him what he had decided. He tried to explain that he was fine, and I reminded him that he had to start going to AA by June 18th or move out. This time, I had given him a deadline. I told him that me and the kids are "done" and don't want him around if he planned to continue drinking.

He returned to the sofa in the basement. I then realized I had made 'Father's Day', his deadline.

Damn!

He was a mess again on Sunday. I went downstairs again at supper time as I hadn't seen him again all day. He wasn't even trying. I had been outside, sunbathing to increase my vitamin D, as the day was warm and beautiful from dusk on. I hoped he had eaten at some point but wasn't sure. He made a comment that he wasn't feeling well, and his eyes were bloodshot, glassy and he looked as though he had been drinking. He picked at his dinner, and later went to change his clothes for the first time that weekend. He walked a bit in the backyard, and Abby almost convinced him to drive to Chelmsford to get her an ice cream but I told them both that he wasn't feeling well and should not drive in this state. She had slept throughout dinner, so she wasn't aware of his current status when she asked.

On Monday, while in bed, I received a text from Mark two floors down, that he was staying home from work. I received another text from Abby, one floor down, that she had a headache. I brought Abby some ibuprofen and shortly thereafter heard Ian calling me, to complain about a pain in his abdomen. All three of them stayed home, and I left early for the YMCA. I went to have a hot tub, before the Aquafit class. It was honestly, the start of a very positive day for me!

I made my way to my class for 9:00, and my friend, neighbour and book buddy, Joanne showed up to join me for class. Afterwards, I walked down Durham street from the YMCA, to a local tea shop called "Tea & Bloom" for a Matcha tea with a little honey, and walked back to the car. I went to the Cancer Centre for my pre-Denosumab injection bloodwork to make sure my calcium levels were still in good shape. While there, the phlebotomist, taking my blood was Nada, whom I recognized from when I first started working at the hospital lab. I briefed her on my current state of health and she gave me a hug and told me she really wanted to give me something. She said she has a ladybug to give me for good luck but she wanted me to come back as she didn't have any on her. Being that I just created a "strong box" for all of my tokens of luck and well wishes for my journey, I looked forward to adding that symbol and that moment to my collection.

My coworker and I had arranged to meet for lunch, so he was at the cancer centre looking for me. When we found one another, Jim gave me a big hug and told me that I looked great. Jim gave the greatest hugs. He was one of my closest friends at work. He had a great energy about him and a very positive outlook on life. He left his vehicle at work, which was just next to the hospital, and came with me to my car. He treated me to lunch, and we chatted for a half hour before placing our lunch order. He had had his own difficult journey of late, and I was happy that I could be there for him, as he had been for me. After our two-hour lunch, it was time to go home and check on the downtrodden.

The vibration in my car had just started a couple of days before, and was becoming significant as I pulled into our driveway. At the same time, it occurred to me that while I was recovering, Mark had put new tires on my car...I got out and found two lug nuts loose on the front tire of the drivers' side. I tightened them by hand, and hopped back in the car, heading to a garage.

I'm sure that our Maker had a hand in this moment, as the mechanic who grabbed the wrench to tighten the lug nuts, was the man that used to carpool with Mark to the AA meetings a couple of years ago. To respect his anonymity, I will call him "Sam". I briefed Sam while I was there and he took his time to describe the thought process of an alcoholic, which sounded like no thought process at all. He asked me to wait and took off at a half run towards a truck that was just getting ready to leave. The truck made a large turn around to meet me off to the side, where I was parked. This truck belonged to a man who was an old friend of Mark's from the days when he used to own a racehorse. He was also a more recent friend at the AA meetings as he was a recovering alcoholic as well, so with respect to anonymity, I will call him "Perry". The three of us discussed both sides of the addiction and the men conspired to make Mark go with them to the meeting in Lively that night.

Perry sent a couple of texts off to Mark, and told me he would be at the house for 6:15. He also gave me his cell number and asked me to let him know what kind of state Mark was in, as going to the meeting might be futile if he was 'half-in-the-bag' (drunk). I gave him a hug before we separated and I was filled with hope and gratitude for the forces that made us all show up there at that time, on that day.

The hope gave me a little excitement and I performed a little dance as I shared the good news with both kids, whom had recovered from their ills that day. I made sure to bring Mark my leftover pizza from lunch, to check on him and make sure he had some food in his belly. Every time, I went downstairs he was sleeping on the couch. I'd woken him a couple of times and after asking five times if he had eaten that day, he never replied. He just looked at me blankly. He wanted pity.

I made soup, meatloaf, potatoes and veggies for an early supper, so that Mark could be fed, before the meeting. I went downstairs to tell him that supper was ready and he appeared to nod that he would be coming, but his plate remained unused, as me and the kids finished our meals.

I encouraged the kids to leave the men to their visit as they had followed me and Perry to the family room when he arrived at 6:15. It only took 15 minutes of talking and a pool game and Perry convinced Mark to join him for the meeting. By 6:30, Perry appeared at the top of the stairs followed by Mark. He didn't look at me as he passed through the kitchen but before closing the door, Perry shouted to us, "See you later!".

They both climbed into the truck, and went to the AA meeting. I was so relieved, as I took in a little shimmer of light in with my big meditative breath before I exhaled. As much as I was uplifted to have outside help, I also feared that it was not Mark admitting that he needed help nor was he attending AA of his own volition.

Mark was more chipper when he arrived home at 9:15 p.m. I was in bed with the heat pack on my back. I was trying to stay awake to hear Ian return from his soccer game, but I had a headache and a backache and felt so drained. I did acknowledge him when he came up to the bedroom and told him that Ian wasn't home yet, and that I was very tired. He went to sit out in the backyard. I hoped that meant these efforts made a difference today. I thanked God for that day, and hoped for more of them. I heard Ian come home, and he came up to hear how things had gone that night while he was at his soccer game. Then we were both able to go to sleep.

Perry sent me the following text:

> *"You can't let up on him. Any excuse is a good excuse. He is playing poor Mark.*
>
> *When he starts playing poor Jan and poor kids believe him.*
>
> *We have all been nice. I hate to say it but we have to be tough so he can toughen up.*
>
> *Look after yourself and the kids.*
>
> *You know your situation. Teach the kids for the future.*

I am not trying to be negative. But Mark has a lot of work to do and again unless he embraces this it is not an easy journey.

Keep me posted, I will do what I can.

God bless you, you're a wonderful girl."

I realized that my journey was far from over, but knew we were making progress.

I had been going to the YMCA every morning and the next morning after calling her school to inform them of Abby's vomiting, I kissed Ian and left for the gym. My first class started at 8:00, and it was my second time being a part of this Gentle Fit class. It was a good half hour of strength training using straps attached to the wall, called TRX, and exercises on the mat. I was able to do all of the moves this time. But there was no awkward twisting. I went to the change room to get my swimsuit on and spent some time in the hot tub before my Aquafit class. It was becoming a wonderful start to my days.

Joanne came again to class that morning and loved it, but she had a mishap when her heal landed on the bottom of the pool at just the right angle to embed an earring post into her foot. I meant to go easy but I felt energetic and capable and did more twisting motions in this class. I wondered if I would pay for it that night. Ever since I had started at the YMCA, my back had been so achy early in the morning and so I could no longer lie down for the entire night. I had to sit up, put the heat pack on and meditate.

On my way home, I picked up an electrolyte drink for Abby to help settle her stomach. I walked into her room and was taken aback that Mark was there, laying perpendicular to her. She followed me out of her room afterwards and she wanted to share that she thought her Dad was trying to apologize. I told her that was really a good step, because perhaps he was acknowledging that he had a problem. Abby went upstairs to watch TV and we heard the timer on Mark's phone going off. It was in the kitchen, and I had no clue as to how to shut it off. I brought the noisy phone to Mark to see if he could silence it. He raised his head slightly from Abby's bed with a bewildered look. I asked him the same question about four times and he didn't appear to comprehend. His eyes were red, glassy and bulging out of his head. I turned and left for the kitchen as coincidentally the timer stopped on its own. A few minutes later, I heard the large crash of Abby's belongings that were on her bed, as they fell to the floor when Mark moved. From my vantage point in the kitchen, I saw him stagger to the patio door to let Charlie in. Every step was followed by a wavering pause before the next foot found the floor. He turned and walked to the kitchen where I was. I folded my arms and said "Are you trying to kill yourself?", followed by a reminder, "If this continues, you'd better have a place for Sunday!"

He didn't say a word and returned to his basement post. I went out on the deck with my tea and headphones, and texted Perry. Perry said he doesn't suggest this often, but he really thought Mark was a good candidate for the Rehabilitation Program. We found out that he could not go to Rehab while intoxicated, so Detox was the only first choice... again. I asked Perry if he would help me to get Mark there as I had needed reinforcements the first time. I had to find one more man, and went looking for close neighbours. Two were out of town for the day, but I was able to borrow Joanne's husband, Dermott (Derm). I hoped this would go easier than the last time. Mark's bag was packed and the cavalry came over for 12:30.

We went downstairs altogether to wake up Mark. He was spaced out and defensive. He was adamant that he did not want to go. It was just as hard as the last time. With a half an hour of pleading and reasoning, I finally got pissed off. He resisted me as I tried to put his sandals on, so I cried in a large blubbering sob, "JUST GO!", and started to push him off the couch. In an instant both Perry and Derm were called to action and floated Mark up the stairs to the outside step. When he still refused to put shoes on to walk on our gravel driveway, they dragged him to the truck and pushed him into the backseat of Derm's truck. I asked Joanne if she would stay with Abby, and I climbed in the front seat next to Derm. Perry sat in the back with Mark. He mumbled a little, and argued about going back for his cell phone, and that he wouldn't stay at detox. I directed Derm to the Withdrawal Management Services, off Pine Street.

Derm physically supported Mark as we walked to the entrance. He was still without shoes as he defiantly refused to put them on. We got into the first set of doors and had to ring for the second. This thought brought me back to when I had to pee and we were parked outside of a brothel. I didn't recognize the man who greeted us this time. He articulated to Mark that he can leave of his own free will but that if he were to leave that afternoon in the state he was in, they would call the police. He could be a danger to himself or others. He further said that he would also call me, if Mark were to leave. We said our goodbyes, and Mark and I sobbed together as I hugged him and whispered to him that he could do this. Derm and I left and Perry stayed to give him some friendly encouragement. Perry had to guide him to sit back down as he made his way out to leave with us. Derm walked with me in arm, I thanked him, and he said he was sorry that I had to go through this. I was so relieved to see Perry walking towards us, alone.

I thanked and hugged Perry for his help that day before he left the house. Abby was a little shaken. Ian wasn't home but I told him when he got home and he said "Mom, I'm so sorry that you had to go through this!". I took the kids out for dinner at the Doghouse, after I spent some time at the lake. Ian held my hand as we walked to the restaurant. Our conversations were light. I noticed I had a couple of missed calls from an unknown caller while there. I assumed it was Mark. I was in no rush to speak with him.

Mark called again when I was sitting on the patio with Dad, to ask me to visit the next day, and bring his pre-gabalin for his leg pain, some headache pills, his toothbrush and his cell phone so that he could come outside with me and check his emails. I wished he could just go to rehab after detox. I was told that he would have to arrange it and have a screening interview first, and that it wouldn't happen right after detox. I wanted to stick with my tough love and ask him to find somewhere else to stay once he was ready to leave the program, as he would only stay 3-5 days. He had not acknowledged that he was having a drinking problem nor had he made any attempts to improve things of his own free will. I forced all of this on him. I needed him to know this time how serious I was. Perry had a few very supportive texts following that adventure, and helped me decide to stay on track.

Perry>

> *You have to chase this. He is lying to himself and everyone else.*
>
> *Complete denial.*
>
> *The disease has got him so bad.*
>
> *I tried to look tough yesterday but I choked back tears about 3 times.*
>
> *I have never experienced someone this bad that wasn't a street person.*
>
> *Battle on.*

It was the best sleep that I had in days, that first night. In the morning, Ian was a mess for lack of sleep. He said he had been watching the clock until 3:00 am. I let him crawl back in bed and called his school. Abby managed to get her bus that morning, but had to text me to click "publish" on a web page she had been working on for a presentation that day. The new information disappeared and was irretrievable before I could save it. Shortly after 8:00, a large, black suburban pulled on our driveway, and Mark was dropped off. Son of a biscuit box!

He was coherent but in a frantic state. The first thing he said was "I'm going back! I just need to fill this prescription and get cleaned up. Did Sandra call you?" Sandra, is our work partner and camp partner's wife, who is a nurse at the hospital and was working that particular night shift.

On his first night of detox at around 11:00, he was discharged by ambulance as Mark thought he was having a heart attack. He stayed overnight, and the ER did bloodwork, Electrocardiograms (ECGs) and monitoring. The discharge papers indicated that he had been vomiting blood and had black stools. That wasn't good. Mark was hungry, and started to eat a hardboiled egg that I had in the fridge. He almost immediately started to wretch and wouldn't go directly to the toilet. Instead, he felt compelled to walk around threatening to spew all over the main floor. His upper torso convulsed like a rooster getting ready to blurt out it's morning call. He hacked some mucus, and ran away from the toilet to do the same wretched dance, a few more times. I gave him the last electrolyte drink that we had and instructed him to sip at it. He then wanted a coffee or a pop as he needed caffeine. I made him a coffee in a takeout cup and grabbed our things and we went to the pharmacy to fill the prescription for two new drugs. One for the cravings which also targeted nerve pain, and another for heartburn. He paced while I waited for his prescription. Once we were back in the car and on our way to detox, he was slapping his hand on his left breast. He said, "this is a lot harder this time!". I grimaced and told him, "Remember that!".

I was relieved that he willingly re-admitted himself to the Detox program, and while talking with the intake worker, the topic of a Rehab program came up, and so I asked him to find out what he could and to seriously consider it. He fought back a few sobs and we had a few hugs. I left without a struggle. I got to the YMCA, and had a hot tub and got ready for the second water workout class, "Aqualite", only to find out that it was no longer offered. I was having a lot of pain in my lower back and hips, so perhaps I was meant to take a break. In the meantime, Abby was trying to reach me as she was having an emotional day. One of her classmates did their presentation on cancer and it struck a chord. She fled the classroom in tears. I reached out to Mom to pick her up as I still needed to pop in to work and to go for my monthly Denosumab shot for bone density. I had a hard time calming my head and opted for a long walk alone. I updated Perry:

Perry >

Just on a spot on the lake where I get reception.

Maybe he will figure out he doesn't want to die.

He needs help. Let's not let up on him.

You have become the little sister I never had. And you thought your luck was bad before.

Keep plugging on Jan.

Mark called late that afternoon and I commented that it was the longest conversation we had in weeks. I also brought up the Rehab again, and he said he had just fallen because I got sick. I told him, "Well, I'm going to get sick again, and THIS cannot happen again." He said he understood, but I still felt he still didn't really get it. I resigned to focus on my happiness, from them on. And happiness did not involve living with a time bomb.

The next morning, I reached out for information about the Alcohol Rehabilitation Program at the Camillus Centre, in Elliott Lake. They told me it was a 21-day program and could take four to six weeks to get in, that you first need to have a counsellor complete your drug and alcohol assessment tools and fax that to them to begin the process but it all had to be of Mark's doing. I then called his cousin Denis, to explain what I was trying to accomplish and would he and Lily be willing to house Mark after detox until he could get into the Rehab program. Denis said he would without hesitation as Mark had been so good to them.

That morning, I brought Mark his requested treats of chips and Pepsi, his last prescription for heartburn and the Rehab information. When he said he would come home on Saturday, I finally chose a side of the fence and sternly, but calmly said, “No. You will stay with Denis and Lily until you’ve been through this Rehab program, then you can come home.” He fidgeted uncomfortably, “I’m NOT going to Elliott Lake. There are day programs.” He would find out more while he was there. I was apprehensive about a day program. Mark always looked for shortcuts.

I touched base with my new big brother, Perry.

Perry>

Don’t want to muck up your day but, I talked to someone who is in the know and for the day

program someone has to be in a safer state of mind than Mark is.

He thinks he can do it but he was on that road before and he nearly died.

My friend that I spoke to knows Mark from the group. He is willing to help. But Mark must go the big route. No shortcuts.

Sorry for you, but say no.

Facts are facts.

Still here for you here’s a hug.

The kids seemed to get it. They weren’t obviously emotional in any way. I was also pleased that Ian had talked openly to our favourite teacher, Monsieur Viau, when he took him aside to inquire what was going on with his Dad. I had texted him that he was in hospital and to let me know how much we owed him to treat the class to pizza as Mark had promised to do.

On Friday, I brought Abby and Charlie with me for the afternoon visit with Mark. He wanted the kids and the dog to come, but Ian didn’t feel comfortable with going, and chose to go swimming at his friend Travis’ house instead.

The visiting hour was from 1:30-2:30, and Mark said that he would not be permitted outside to see the dog until 2:00. It was getting to be a muggy day, so I arrived for 1:50 and left all windows and the sunroof window open a few inches. For the short visit, we had in the building, we were pleasantly surprised to hear how Mark acknowledged that he had a problem and that he would have to work on it for the rest of his life. He acknowledged that he was dishonest to Abby when she had confronted him and said he realized what he had done wrong the last time he went through AA. Out of the 12 steps of Alcoholics Anonymous, he only got as far as the first step, to admit that alcohol had the upper hand over him and his life was no longer manageable. He read each of the remaining eleven steps to Abby and I and tried to keep his emotions at bay. It was the most I had heard him speak in months. He said he planned to get a sponsor this time and he would go through Rehab, though he wanted me to go the day program with him to find out whether it was an acceptable alternative to the 21-day program in Elliott Lake. Abby and I both were moved by his apparent determination this time. When I arrived to pick him up the next day, he asked to drive as he worried how I might react when he said what he wanted to say. He confessed that our visit the day before was a very hard day for him. When he looked at me, he said with some difficulty "I forgot about, YOU!" He also noticed changes in the kids that he was too blind to see for some time. He was determined to make things right for all of us.

The kids were getting support. I was getting support. Mark had no choice but to get the help that he needed. I wasn't really letting go, and I wasn't really leaving. I was making him change.

Although it was still to be a journey of moguls, I committed to taking the stance of tough love, and hoped my health would hold long enough to get through this last step and keep Mark in the light.

CHAPTER TWELVE

A New Beginning

He had a great day he said, when the dog and I visited him in Elliott Lake. He had signed himself up for the detox at the Camillus Centre so that he would be the first in line if there was a "no show", on the Monday. Otherwise, it would have been an extra four to six weeks away from home. I wasn't letting him back until he completed the rehabilitation program.

That particular Sunday, he also had Corbin, Lisa and her husband Dean, pay him a visit. It meant a great deal to him.

When we were alone later that afternoon, he asked "What about us?". I had to interrupt my automatic response that erupted before I could stop it "what about us?", and immediately followed up to say "When you are finished the program, you can come home. We will need to start dating again, though." Mark expressed how good it was to hear those words. He was still under the impression that I didn't want him home before September. This thought was likely from our conversation about my needing a break anyway and was okay with being apart for that duration.

As much as it provided a much-needed break and time to heal, I really was looking forward to having him home again. I realized that I could manage just fine without him, but I looked forward to getting reacquainted with the new and improved, Mark.

My social worker didn't think that I wanted him back. She didn't say so directly, but hinted that I hadn't really thought it through yet. I would not be influenced by her 'opinion' on this matter. My autobiography journey through my many journals and the writing process proved to me what was important. I stopped seeing the social worker because I didn't feel that she understood me.

I was finding my strength and self-love and aligned my mind with the decision that if he should fall again while I am still breathing, I would not take him back a third time. I'm strong but I needed to set limits, for my happiness and longevity. A girl has only so much energy and so many cheeks to turn, after all!

My reformed husband settled into a slightly new routine. I got our adjustable split king bed, so each of us had a twin mattress that could be individually controlled. At night he would elevate his head, and get comfy with the television (TV) application (app) on his cell phone and a headset on, so he wouldn't keep me up. He would do his daily reading or meditate, with his new "Headspace" app on his phone for a short, guided meditation.

He went to his AA meetings a couple of times per week, and continued to search for an AA Sponsor. He seemed quite disappointed that Perry declined when he asked him to take on the role. He continued to drink the 0.5% beer, in a sleeve to hide the label. He said he wanted to walk more. He spent a little less time downstairs. I told him that I was available to walk every night.

Work was busy and he often missed lunch, or came home stressed out. I reminded him that his health was more important than work and that he had to set at least a half an hour aside when he could eat lunch, go for a walk or meditate just to tare the weight on his brain.

He came home one day, frazzled. He had backed the truck into a pole. Little things caused us alarm and extra scrutiny as we wanted to make sure he was not regressing to his old ways. I told the kids to stop policing him, as if he felt that he was being blamed for something that he wasn't doing, he might give up the fight and resume his drinking, out of spite.

Abby was great in accepting him back and treating him like her father. They had their discussions, but she remained respectful. Ian was very protective of me. He struggled with trusting his Dad to not fall off the wagon again. Ian kept to himself mostly, and often went to spend a good part of most days at his friend's, and playing soccer, or playing games on his phone or online. He started hiding empty pop cans in the locations that he used to find his Dad's empty booze stashes. When Mark asked where he learned that, Abby and I looked at each other knowingly and Abby told him, that Ian likely learned it from you, Dad. She was becoming so adult, so quickly.

I continued to feel pretty good and was getting ready to integrate more exercises at the gym. I thought that if my muscles were strong, I'd be less prone to injury. After my bone- and cat-scans in June, the Oncologist forbade me to do any lifting and to only partake in water exercises. I had fractured another vertebra. I suspected that it was from the mat exercises in the gentle fit class. This one was positioned higher on my back, my T8. This was not as painful as the burst fracture to my T11, the previous spring, which was only millimeters from my spine. My tumour markers were decreasing, which I expected due to my improved mobility and reduced pain. I was "living with cancer", not "dying of it", which made coping so much better for the family. They were given time to process and come to terms with my mortality.

It came to my realization that going back to work would be detrimental to my health, and decided it was time to apply for long term sick leave. This was going to be my retirement. "Freedom 45!", is how I termed my new status. I much preferred to stay positive and to say "I'm dying", was not an option for me. In fact, I was starting to feel happier and healthier than I have ever felt. I felt a new peace taking over. I had been given the gift of the "present", to share my love and help mend the wounds that had been detrimental to my family. We were a team after all, and no matter what, we tend to be the toughest on those we love. When we scrape away conversations fueled only by ego, then we uncover the unconditional love beneath. A love for not only one another, and the powers that be, but a self-love.

Meditation also helped me achieve this peace and smooth away the roughness that can sometimes trigger our nerves to awaken the opportunistic ego.

I would catch myself singing to the silly song, "If I was you, I'd wanna be me too!" I sing it with a giggle and some sass, not to say that I was boasting but I am happy with how my journey has gone.

It has reconnected me with my brother, solidified my self-respect, opened up the hearts of strangers that I manage to engage in conversation, and made my days so much more valuable to me. It gave me the psychological infrastructure that supported me as I spread my wings.

I loved the thoughts that played through my head, reminiscent of when Mark and I were just friends and I was wanting more. I was right back there, trying to juggle, tip toe and ease comfortably back into our good times again together. Every day that went by, brought me closer to my husband. I started planning how our first sexual encounter would play out, but it wouldn't happen until I felt ready and strong enough to not break, during the process.

As we were alone together in the kitchen one day, I gave him a 10 second hug to get his attention. Only 10 seconds though, as 20 seconds may have activated the "gonna get lucky" process. I looked him in the eye and was happy to have his attention, and said, "I think we need to converse together more, as I feel that sometimes we aren't understanding the intentions behind what we may say or do. For example, when I bought you the T-shirt which read "More handsome, than handy!", I thought you would recognize that being 'handy' is not your forté but you would be comfortable in laughing about that part and at the same time be flattered by the fact that I'm calling you 'handsome'." I realized that laughing at oneself was not a common value to all people. Secondly, at night he would place an extra pillow between us. I was inclined to see it as a barrier or blockade to avoid me, but his intention in his pillow placement was to shelter me from the light of his phone app. He found comfort in falling asleep with the TV on. We both had to learn to not make any assumptions about the others' intended meaning when we spoke. I had to teach him to open up, and for us to get to know each other again.

He was trying so hard and I was becoming very protective of him and the kids. So much so, that I needed to talk to Dad about stepping back and letting me do my thing.

Dad was always there as a sounding board. Sometimes I could just let go of some of his comments when he regressed to the parent role and criticized Mark or the kids for living by different rules or not pulling their weight. He said "they should be cherishing you right now!" I understood his concern, but I know my family loves me, and needs me, and I needed time to help them get to where they need to be. To find their strengths and process the life hurdles in the healthiest manner, without being criticized or judged as they grieve and grow. Dad was accustomed to immediate gratification. He never did anything slowly or lazily. He grew up in a difficult time where your well-being depended so much more on following the essential rules for survival. He didn't understand Mark, but he loved him.

One day, I was out for dinner with Abby, and she asked me to give her a ride to the curling club early the next morning. I told her I would drive her and asked if her Mixed Doubles partner would need a ride too. I had some difficulty waking up some mornings due to the cannabis oil that I took at night, so I decided to ask for Dad's help. I texted him to ask if he'd drive Abby to the club. He said "no problem". My next text was to ask if he wouldn't mind also picking up her (male) Mixed Doubles partner at the University. His response made me see red.

Dad> "Abby I will. Her partner can find his own way."

After I told Abby I could drive them both, he said 'no'. I texted him back to say "Never mind, I'll drive them". I had to snuff the automatic response that wanted so much to be insulted, angry and disrespectful.

Dad didn't take it well at first as his reasoning was fueled by his love and desire to protect me. I was tactful, and texted him later to say:

Me> "I understand that everything you do is with my best interest in mind. I know that you love me and just want to protect me. But, I am an adult and can make decisions that I think is best for me. Being constantly challenged on that course is very stressful for me. Thank-you for being here, but I don't need you to parent at this time, while I am qualified and able. I love you and yes, I was frustrated last night. I will get over it."

Dad stayed to himself most of that day. I knew he would be taking offence and consider moving out as he could to be dramatic, and irrational at times. So, I went downstairs to see him. He was cuddled up in front of the fireplace watching some TV series on the Roku box connected to the TV, drowning his sorrows in a glass of red wine. He seemed relieved that we spoke like normal and he apologized for interfering. We hugged and I told him that he was forgiven and that I understood his concerns. He still decided to give me some space and went to spend some time with his girlfriend Cathy, in Ottawa.

Meanwhile, my days started getting a bit too full as I kept taking on new projects, my version of a bucket list. Not only was I making jewelry and toxin free toiletries, but I also started an online group called "Jan's DIY Basics", to teach and learn with others about making our own toiletries and cosmetics, and reducing waste.

I started "JANSQUEST" blog to identify the hurdles in our social services causing roadblocks to individuals needing assistance. My blogging process led me to attending a 'Bridges out of Poverty' seminar at our local health unit, after which, I was contacted to become an Ally for the "Circles and Allies" program to aid those in poverty wanting help to get on their feet. I justified this as my "Bucket List Quest", as a Bucket List Vacation didn't seem as rewarding to me. Plus, with my sleep habits, I had become dependent on cannabis oil to stay asleep all night. It was the only thing that would subdue my bone pain and quiet my mind, without causing any side effects. If I were to travel and not bring it, I would not sleep and I would therefore be in pain. This was not an option. Instead, I wanted to surround myself with those I care about and do the things that I love. I really had been given the gift of the present.

I started noticing little things that I interpreted as signs that were guiding me in my journey. Affirmations that I needed to stay the course. An example was the evening that Mark raced home to drop off Charlie and pick up Abby to go curling at the Idylwylde. I was hoping to have finished making a salve for one of our club friends, but they were too quick. After about an hour, I decided to go anyway, and watch their game. On my way, I remembered that I needed a couple of things from the natural health store, so I made a pit stop. As I pulled up to Paris Natural Foods, I found a young man, in his late 20's or early 30's, sitting on the cold concrete with his back to the building, a sign asking for donations and a dirty sleeping bag and pillow on the side. As soon as my headlights found him, and I put the truck in park and turned off the engine, I knew that I was supposed to be there. I had an interview with him and he let me take a photo as long as he could hide his face. His name was Phil, and he was very coherent, articulate and kind. He explained that he was just trying to raise $100, so that he could make the deposit on an apartment to get a receipt that he could bring to Ontario Works to prove that he had an address. He believed that he needed an address in order to access assistance. It was then that my quest got absolute focus. I needed to teach others about the population living on the streets and perhaps create a movement. Perhaps together, we could educate those on the street that have experienced such frustration as they attempt to navigate the system. I wanted to end homelessness.

I found the meaning of my life in the most unsuspecting circumstances. I was meant to be someone special, whether it is only to a few people, or to the general population. I knew that I would not have a "happy ever after", I would do my darndest to make it so for my family.

Empowerment of my children, a more positive mindset and a love for the little things in life constitute the legacy that I want to leave when I'm needed elsewhere by the powers that be.

Faith
Belief
Hope
Love
Forgiveness
Empathy
These are the qualities that will save us from ourselves.
Perhaps, this had been my special destiny all along. To teach my little universe the many colours, and healing strength of love.
Love Jan
xoxo

Acknowledgements

It is a very difficult thing to put your most private thoughts, experiences and life out there to be read, discussed and perhaps judged. Like friendships, I feel you have to jump in with both feet and take the chance, or you don't show your true self. This can also make you vulnerable to be hurt, but any worthwhile relationship is worth the risk. Sometimes, we have to hurt. Pain in life, can make us stronger and help us in our future decisions. Sometimes, we nurture our children too much to avoid them pain. Hurt is a natural part of being human, and we shortchange them of some important building blocks for their independence.

It is best to make choices that you don't think you will regret. Regrets tie you down and become obstacles in your emotional freedom and inward journey. I feel blessed to have been comfortable to first share this endeavour with my younger sister. Melanie, Mel, Shmoe. She was on her own journey but always had time to give feedback on each Chapter that I shared with her on Google Docs. Sometimes she'd reach out to discuss certain things that she hadn't known, and though we may have had some laughs and tears through the course of his project, she never made me embarrassed or made me feel judged for it. For her support, I will be forever grateful. I think this book has really brought us closer.

My cousin, Timothy had a role to play in this book, and I really wanted to consult with him, before publishing anything. He has always been supportive and has become quite well versed and articulate in his forties, so I must say a big thank-you for his input!

I have to mention the Linda from 'Be Come One', in Wasaga, with whom I first felt comfortable to face my demons and look objectively at my life situation. It was this session that became the turning point in my life's direction.

One of the lessons that my husband taught me was the value of friendship. Being with him, allowed me to spread my wings, network and cultivate many wonderful friendships. These friends played such a prominent role in the foundation of my strength. From being there to listen, to offering their time or support, to just making me feel cared for and giving me a hug, when I needed it. He also made me realize that some life rules are very valuable. We all have our own rules to live by, and these rules shape our expectations of others.

My divorced parents have far fewer expectations of one another now, than they did when they were married. They are unhindered to love each other as family and life-long friends. As much as my friends have been the foundation of my strength, my parents and family have been the rock below, which supported that foundation. They have been there through the good times and bad. I credit them for their strength in holding back when they wanted so much to set everything right. They were there to catch me when I fell. I could depend on them when I needed it most. I'm so fortunate that they were so healthy and able when I was weak.

My co-workers were very supportive and became an extension of my family. Some drove me crazy like siblings do, but when the going got tough, even the most unlikely supporters were there for me. Thank-you Doreen, Fran, Jim, Deanna, Sue, Alicia, Dave, Tammy, Rosanne, Alicia, Sophie and Lorraine.

My neighbours and 'The Lakeside Book Buddies' were my saving grace and loving 'Sistas'! These women showed me true friendship and love. I finally had friends of my own. I will forever hold them in dearest regard, Colette, Joanne, Monique, Deanna, Debbie, Danielle, Donna, Parisa, Cathy, Linda and Holly.

My childhood friends, and in particular Kristi, who was a contributing part of who I became and in my time of need, reached out to me and sent me strength from so far away. Thanks to you and Sabina for helping with my 'mana'.

My new big brother, "Perry", 'was sent to us for a reason. I'm so glad that I bumped into him on that day in June, when I needed more strength to fight Mark's demons. And he stuck with me when the going got tough. It was meant to be, and we will most definitely keep in touch.

I cannot omit a huge "Thank-you!" from the bottom of my heart to those caring souls that have been praying for me and my health since my diagnosis in early 2017. I specifically want to thank Muffie and the lovely souls at St. Andrew's Church. Connie and Faye, my childhood dental assistants, in Sudbury, and those wonderful individuals at the Salvation Army, in Dildo, NFLD. I feel truly beholden, that you have taken the time to send me such positive energy. Please don't stop, as I'm feeling wonderful and have much to do, before I sign out. It must be working. Bless you all!

With no doubt, my children, Abby and Ian, were my reasons for everything! I don't agree with always putting one's spouse first. A child's welfare should be the priority of both parents, until the children have their own wings. It was their frustration, disappointment and feeling of loss from their father's affliction that brought out the Momma Bear strength in me. I could finally take a stand with their Dad to shock him enough with the ultimate choice after Detox, of seeking proper help before he could move back in. I do not wish for my children to ever feel responsible for the difficulties in our marriage, as I felt with my parents. Grownups are just big kids that make choices. Some good, some bad. I wanted to be open with our children as they will strengthen and learn from this process and hopefully make good choices in their own lives. If I beat the odds and become a long term METAvivor, it will be because my children gave the will and determination to stay on this earth for them. If I succumb, it will be because I earned my wings and God needed me earlier. Love you up to the sky and back down again! And Ian, I love you through a frog!

Moving Forward

Feelings, where did you go?
I knew you once, a long time ago.
Embracing you may frighten me
Will avoidance of you, set me free?
I awaken to my inner voice
Consumed by the imminent choice
Breathe to find the secret plan
Do I really want to keep this man?
He sees me now, he is more present
But, I no longer know him, though he's pleasant
He uses words, I so longed to hear
But I no longer trust, that his meaning is dear
Perhaps, we start over? What do we do?
You get to know me and I get to know you.
Ask me on a date. Pick from the jar.
The kids gave us ideas, no need to go far
Remember to be patient, right from the start
When trying to mend the pieces of my heart
May the challenges we have had to survive
Make a deeper connection and a love that will thrive.

Jan-Andrea Day

Commentary

Never Doubt Perry:

I could not find his exact wording, from the time he first told me, but when I told 'Perry', that I had named him so, in this book, he said it was funny that I had picked that name. Growing up, he had a friend, by that very name, who was very bright. When talking politics, he asked Perry what 'NDP' stood for. The real Perry did not say the "New Democratic Party", but instead he said "Never Doubt Perry". Years later, this same Perry was a pilot of a small bush plane, when it had engine troubles and crash landed. Perry managed to save everyone on board, and walked away from the crash. This made 'my Perry' recall to "Never Doubt Perry"! 'My Perry' has been invaluable to me and to my family. I will never doubt you, and will be forever grateful for your support! Love Jan

"Just finished it. I'm blown away...Strength does not even begin to describe you. It is superhuman strength and unwavering compassion. It's late here and I have work tomorrow, but I will fall asleep thinking about the glowing energy radiating from beside a frozen lake in Azilda, Half a planet away. Your healing journey is a beacon of what is possible and what really matters. Thank you so much." Kristiann Allen

Note: Many names have been altered, for the respect of those that would like privacy. It is my story, and as such, everything herein is from my eyes, and my memory. I'm not sure how long I have, so I wanted this published while I am still here. I hold no one responsible for the choices that I have made, I just wanted to explain to the kids, what I was like and hopefully, my story will play in the background as they make their life choices.

May you be free to create yourselves and always choose to be positive. You are bound to have hurdles in your lives, but the only thing in your power, is how you react and deal to these hurdles.

Follow the light.

With every copy sold, 5% of net royalties will be awarded to the METAvivor research, in hopes of finding a cure for Metastatic Breast Cancer. Thank-you for your support! With much love and positivity!

Jan-Andrea Day